THE IMPACT
OF THE
GDPR
ON THE
ONLINE ADVERTISING
MARKET

ISBN:
978-3-9824173-0-1 *Paperback*
978-3-9824173-1-8 *Amazon eBook*
978-3-9824173-3-2 *eBook*
978-3-9824173-2-5 *Interactive PDF*

Contact details: Bernd Skiera (skiera@skiera.de).
Prof. Dr. Bernd Skiera, Department of Marketing, Faculty of Economics and Business, Goethe-University Frankfurt am Main, Theodor-W.-Adorno-Platz 4, 60629 Frankfurt, Germany, Phone +49-69-798-34649, Fax: +49-69-798-35001, email: skiera@wiwi.uni-frankfurt.de.

Book Website: www.gdpr-impact.com

This project received funding from the European Research Council (ERC) under the European Union's Horizon 2020 research and innovation program (grant agreement No. 833714).

European Research Council
Established by the European Commission

THE IMPACT
OF THE
GDPR
ON THE
ONLINE ADVERTISING
MARKET

BERND SKIERA, KLAUS MILLER, YUXI JIN,
LENNART KRAFT, RENÉ LAUB, JULIA SCHMITT

Abstract

In an effort to protect users' privacy, regulators all over the world are introducing new laws that impose restrictions on firms' capacity to collect and process personal data. These restrictions substantially affect the online advertising industry, in which publishers and advertisers rely on user data to personalize ads and content and to generate revenue. To comply with the new privacy-related obligations they face, firms have had to change their operations profoundly, incurring substantial costs related to the development of technical and legal infrastructure, as well as day-to-day processing costs associated with compliance—while at the same time losing revenue as a result of limitations on access to user data. Researchers, practitioners, and policymakers have yet to obtain a comprehensive and precise understanding of these costs, even though such an understanding is crucial for evaluating the economic effects of privacy laws and for shaping future regulations. This book aims to provide such an understanding, focusing on the European General Data Protection Regulation (GDPR) as the first of a handful of strict privacy laws initiated in Europe and worldwide.

Specifically, this book begins by (i) outlining how the online advertising industry operates, and providing a breakdown of how the different actors in this industry—primarily publishers and advertisers—leverage users' personal data to pursue their respective goals. Next, it (ii) provides an overview of the contents of the GDPR, highlighting the aspects that are most meaningful to the advertising industry. In particular, it discusses the need for firms to supply a legal basis for data processing, which, in practice, entails obtaining users' permission to process their data for specified purposes. This book further (iii) provides step-by-step descriptions of the complex process of obtaining user permission for data processing, elaborating on the costs involved, and on the tools that have been developed to assist firms in this process. One such tool is the Transparency and Consent Framework (TCF), a framework designed by Europe's Internet Advertising Bureau to standardize the procedures through which firms formulate permission requests and transfer user data to other firms in a manner compliant with the GDPR.

The manuscript also (iv) provides empirical insights into the complexity of the process of obtaining permission for personal data processing, for industry actors as well as for the users who respond to these requests. Notably, our estimates suggest that if, in line with the GDPR's vision to put users in control of their data, users were indeed to make all possible decisions regarding the processing of their personal information, the average user would need to devote, on average, 78 minutes per day to making data processing–related decisions.

Table of Contents

Abstract. v

List of Abbreviations xii

List of Figures xiii

List of Tables. xv

1. Introduction 1

2. Overview of the Online Advertising Industry 5

   2.1 Essential Actors: Advertisers, Publishers and Users. 5

   2.2 Scope and Types of Online Advertising 7

   2.3 Real-Time Bidding as a Process of Selling Online Advertising 8

   2.4 Description of Other Actors. 10

   2.5 Main Takeaways 12

3. User Tracking, Profiling, and Targeting in Online Advertising 15

   3.1 Description of User Tracking Technologies 15

      3.1.1 Single-Device User Tracking 16

         3.1.1.1 Cookies 16

         3.1.1.2 Digital Fingerprinting. .19

         3.1.1.3 Advertising Identifiers .19

         3.1.1.4 Local Storage 20

         3.1.1.5 Tracking Pixel. 20

      3.1.2 Cross-Device User Tracking 20

         3.1.2.1 Cross-Device User Tracking on a First-Party Website 21

         3.1.2.2 Cross-Device User Tracking on a Third-Party Website 21

      3.1.3 Comparison of User Tracking Technologies 21

   3.2 Importance of Tracking, Profiling, and Targeting for
the Online Advertising Industry 24

3.2.1 Importance for Advertisers 25

3.2.2 Importance for Publishers 27

3.3 Implications for Users 28

3.3.1 Personalization of Content 28

3.3.2 Personalization of Ads 29

3.3.3 Privacy 29

3.4 Main Takeaways 30

4. **Personal Data Processing under the GDPR** **31**

4.1 Aim and Scope of the GDPR 31

4.2 Definition of Personal Data 32

4.3 User Rights with Regard to Personal Data Processing 33

4.3.1 Rights Enabling Users to Understand the Processing of Their Personal Data . . . 33

4.3.2 Rights Enabling Users to Change the Processing of Their Personal Data 34

4.3.3 Rights Enabling Users to Restrict the Processing of Their Personal Data 35

4.4 Obligations for Firms that Process Personal Data 36

4.4.1 The Role of the Firm: Data Controller or Data Processor 36

4.4.1.1 Definition of Data Controller 36

4.4.1.2 Definition of Data Processor 36

4.4.1.3 Relationship Between Data Controller and Data Processor 36

4.4.2 Shared Obligations for Both the Data Controller and Data Processor 37

4.4.3 Obligations for Data Controller but not Data Processor 39

4.4.4 Obligations with Respect to Legal Bases 39

4.4.4.1 Legal Bases not Relevant for Advertising 40

4.4.4.1.1 Vital Interest 40

4.4.4.1.2 Public Interest 40

4.4.4.1.3 Legal Obligation 40

4.4.4.1.4 Contract Fulfillment 41

4.4.4.2 Legal Bases Relevant for Advertising 41

4.4.4.2.1 Legitimate Interest 41

4.4.4.2.2 Consent 42

4.5 Specific Conditions Regarding Legal Bases for User Tracking Technologies 43

4.6 Legal Bases for Tracking under other Privacy Laws 44

4.7 Main Takeaways 46

5. **Effects of the Requirement for a Legal Basis for Data Processing** 47

    5.1 Effects Independent of the Outcome of the User's Decision 48

        5.1.1 Effects of Asking for Permission 48

            5.1.1.1 Effects on Firms Operating in the Online Advertising Industry 48

            5.1.1.2 Effects on the User 49

        5.1.2 Effects of Documenting and Managing Permissions. 50

            5.1.2.1 Effects on Firms Operating in the Online Advertising Industry 50

            5.1.2.2 Effects on the User 52

    5.2 Effects Dependent on the Outcome of the User's Decision 53

        5.2.1 Effects of Granting Permission. 53

            5.2.1.1 Effects on Firms Operating in the Online Advertising Industry 53

            5.2.1.2 Effects on the User 53

        5.2.2 Effects of Denying Permission 54

            5.2.2.1 Effects on Firms Operating in the Online Advertising Industry 54

            5.2.2.2 Effects on the User 55

    5.3 Main Takeaways 57

6. **Consent Management Tools** 59

    6.1 Consent Management Platforms (CMPs) for the Online Advertising Industry 59

        6.1.1 Use of Consent Management Platform (CMP) for Requesting
            User Permission for Data Processing. 60

        6.1.2 Use of Consent Management Platform (CMP) for Managing Permission 61

    6.2 Software for the User 63

        6.2.1 Use of Browser Extensions for Making Decisions on Permission. 64

        6.2.2 Use of Browser Extensions for Managing Permissions 66

    6.3 Main Takeaways 66

7. **Getting User Permission for Personal Data Processing via the
Transparency and Consent Framework (TCF)** .67

    7.1 Challenges of Getting Permission. 67

        7.1.1 Challenges of Specifying Purposes for Permission 69

        7.1.2 Challenges of Handling Permission. 70

        7.1.3 Challenges of Checking Permission for Data Transfer 71

    7.2 Transparency and Consent Framework (TCF) .72

    7.3 Mitigating Challenges in Specifying Purposes for Permission 73

        7.3.1 Facilitating Accuracy of Communication 73

7.3.1.1 Purposes 73

7.3.1.2 Special Purposes 75

7.3.2 Facilitating Explicitness of Communication 76

7.3.2.1 Features. 76

7.3.2.2 Special Features 76

7.3.3 Facilitating Convenience of Communication with Stacks 79

7.4 Mitigating Challenges in Handling Permission 80

7.4.1 Facilitating Asking for Permission 80

7.4.1.1 Global Vendor List (GVL) 80

7.4.1.2 Consent Management Platforms (CMPs) Registered with the TCF 81

7.4.2 Facilitating Storing Permission with Transparency and
Consent String (TC String) 82

7.4.3 Integrating Asking for Permission and Storing Permission 83

7.4.3.1 Case 1: A Publisher Obtains Consent on its own Behalf 84

7.4.3.2 Case 2: A Publisher Obtains Consent on Behalf of a Vendor 85

7.4.3.3 Case 3: A Publisher Obtains Consent on Behalf of Multiple Vendors. 87

7.4.3.4 Example Procedures: Concluding Remarks 89

7.5 Mitigating Challenges in Checking Permission for Data Transfer 90

7.5.1 Facilitating Checking Permission for Publishers 90

7.5.2 Facilitating Checking Permission for Data Transfer Between Vendors. 93

7.6 Main Takeaways 94

8. **Empirical Examination of the Complexity of Getting
Permission for Data Processing** **95**

8.1 Aim of the Empirical Study 95

8.2 Data Collection and Description 96

8.3 Examining the Complexity of Getting Permission for Actors
in the Online Advertising Industry 98

8.3.1 Measurement of Complexity: Interconnectedness 98

8.3.2 Description of Results 99

8.4 Examining the Complexity that Users Face in Making Decisions about Permission . 100

8.4.1 Measurement of Complexity: Decision Costs 100

8.4.2 Description of Results 104

8.4.2.1 Number of User Decisions 104

8.4.2.2 Time Spent on Making Decisions. 105

8.5 Main Takeaways 110

9. **Outlook on Further Developments** **111**

    9.1 Activities that Aim to Decrease the Processing of Personal Data 111

    9.2 Activities that Aim to Increase the Processing of Personal Data 113

    9.3 Outlook on Further Regulatory Activities 114

        9.3.1 Digital Services Act 115

        9.3.2 Digital Markets Act 115

        9.3.3 ePrivacy Regulation 116

        9.3.4 Tracking-Free Ads Coalition 117

        9.3.5 Deviations of the GDPR's Interpretation and Enforcement 118

    9.4 Outlook on Further Activities of Consumer Protection Agencies 119

        9.4.1 None of Your Business (NOYB) 119

        9.4.2 Irish Council for Civil Liberties 120

10. **Summary and Conclusions** **121**

    10.1 Summary 121

    10.2 Conclusions 123

11. **References** **125**

12. **Glossary** **131**

13. **Information about the Authors** **139**

    13.1 Bernd Skiera 139

    13.2 Klaus Miller 139

    13.3 Yuxi Jin 139

    13.4 Lennart Kraft 140

    13.5 René Laub 140

    13.6 Julia Schmitt 140

List of Abbreviations

API:	Application Programming Interface
CCPA:	California Consumer Privacy Act
CMP:	Consent Management Platform
CNIL:	Commission Nationale de l'Informatique et des Libertés, i.e., the French Data Protection Agency
CR:	Conversion Rate
CTR:	Click-through Rate
DMA:	Digital Markets Act
DPA:	Data Protection Authority
DSA:	Digital Services Act
DSP:	Demand-side platform
GDPR:	General Data Protection Regulation
GVL:	Global Vendor List (in TCF)
IAB:	Interactive Advertising Bureau
LGPD:	Brazil's privacy law, Lei Geral de Proteção de Dados
LIA:	Legitimate Interests Assessment
NOYB:	None of Your Business
NPO:	Nederlandse Publieke Omroep, which is Netherland's public broadcaster
PDPA:	Thailand's privacy law, Personal Data Protection Act
PDPB:	India's privacy law, Personal Data Protection Bill
PIMS:	Personal Information Management Services
PIPL:	China's privacy law, Personal Information Protection Law
PV:	Publisher-vendor
RTB:	Real-time bidding
SSP:	Supply-side platform
TC string:	Transparency and Consent String (in TCF)
TCF:	Transparency and Consent Framework
UI:	User Interface
WTP	Willingness to pay

List of Figures

Figure 1: Interplay among the Essential Actors of the Online Advertising Market. 6

Figure 2: Size and Share of Different Formats of Online Advertising in the US (IAB 2021) 7

Figure 3: Digital Advertising Spend per Capita in 15 countries (IAB 2020) 8

Figure 4: Illustration of the Auction Process in Real-Time Bidding (RTB). 9

Figure 5: Overview of Actors in the Online Advertising Industry (DisplayLUMAscape) 10

Figure 6: Delivery of Content and Ads from the User's Perspective when Visiting a Website 12

Figure 7: Categorization of User Tracking Technologies 16

Figure 8: Relationship between Tracking, Profiling and Targeting for Online Advertising 24

Figure 9: Forms of Targeting in Online Advertising 25

Figure 10: Example of a Cookie Banner (here: www.ecodibergamo.it) 48

Figure 11: Example of a Data Request (here: Member Area of Zalando.de). 52

Figure 12: Example of the PUR Model (here: www.washingtonpost.com). 56

Figure 13: Managing Cookie Settings at Bloomberg.com 62

Figure 14: Example of a History of a User's Decisions on Permission for Personal Data Processing. 63

Figure 15: Legal Bases for (Special) Purposes and (Special) Features in the Transparency and Consent Framework (TCF) 2.0 78

Figure 16: Process of Getting Consent under the Transparency and Consent Framework (TCF) for Case 1. 84

Figure 17: Process of Asking for and Storing Consent under the Transparency and Consent Framework (TCF) for Case 2 86

Figure 18: Process of Getting Consent under the Transparency and Consent Framework (TCF) for Case 3. 88

Figure 19: Outcomes of Actions from a Publisher, a Vendor, and a User When a Publisher Transfers Data to a Vendor 92

Figure 20: Outcomes of States of Two Vendors When a Vendor Transfers Data to another Vendor. 93

Figure 21: User Interface of the TCF CMP Validator .97

Figure 22: Development of Number of Vendors Participating in the TCF 2.0 98

Figure 23: Histogram of Number of Vendors on the GVL for each
Publisher in the TCF 99

Figure 24: Example of a Publisher Using Stacks to Get User's Permission
(here: theguardian.com) 103

Figure 25: Histogram of Number of User Decisions on Cookie Banner for
each Publisher in Scenario Case Heavy 104

Figure 26: Histogram of Number of User Decisions on Cookie Banner for
each Publisher in Scenario Case Medium 105

List of Tables

Table 1:   Comparison of Most Important User Tracking Technologies 23

Table 2:   Applicability of the GDPR for EU and non-EU Firms
Processing Personal Data of EU and non-EU Citizens 32

Table 3:   Overview of User Rights and Their Aims under the GDPR 33

Table 4:   Overview of Obligations for both Data Controller and Data
Processor under the GDPR. 37

Table 5:   Overview of Obligations only for Data Controller and not for Data Processor . . .39

Table 6:   Comparison of Legal Bases for Tracking in Major Privacy Laws Worldwide 45

Table 7:   Core Functionalities of a Consent Management Platform (CMP) 60

Table 8:   Steps, Actions, and Challenges in Getting User Permission for
Personal Data Processing towards Supplying a Legal Basis under the GDPR . . .68

Table 9:   Specification of Purposes in the Transparency and Consent
Framework (TCF) 2.0 74

Table 10:   Specification of Special Purposes in the Transparency and
Consent Framework (TCF) 2.0 75

Table 11:   Specification of Features in the Transparency and Consent
Framework (TCF) 2.0 76

Table 12:   Specification of Special Features in the Transparency and
Consent Framework (TCF) 2.0 77

Table 13:   Example of a Stack in the Transparency and Consent Framework (TCF) 2.0. . .79

Table 14:   Overview of Cases of Asking for and Storing Consent under
the Transparency and Consent Framework (TCF) 83

Table 15:   Legal Bases for Purposes under TCF Specification of an
Example Vendor (here: Emerse Sverige AB) 91

Table 16:   Example of User Decisions in Case Heavy, Case Medium, and Case Light. . . . 101

Table 17:   Example for Calculating Number of User Decisions on Cookie
Banner Settings for Scenarios Case Heavy, Case Medium, and Case Light . . . 102

Table 18:   Calculation of Content Reading Time and the Number of Daily Visited Websites . 106

Table 19:   Summary of Assumptions for Decision Time Calculation. 107

Table 20:   Calculation of User Decision Time on Cookie Banner in Scenario Case Light . . 108

Table 21:   Summary of User Decision Cost Estimation under Different Scenarios 109

1

Introduction

Tracking technologies such as cookies and digital fingerprinting enable firms to collect and exchange extensive data about consumers ("users"). These data are often used to improve the performance of online advertising, which publishers—here defined as websites or apps that provide space to display ads—rely on to finance the "free" content to which their users have become accustomed. Until recently, such data collection was massive in scope, and often occurred without users' permission, which led to a loss of user privacy. In response, policymakers in Europe and elsewhere have put forward initiatives to protect user privacy. One of the most prominent regulations is Europe's General Data Protection Regulation (GDPR), which went into effect in 2018; this regulation is at the focus of the current book. The GDPR will be complemented by the ePrivacy Regulation (ePR). Outside Europe, large-scale initiatives to protect user privacy include the California Consumer Privacy Act (CCPA), India's Personal Data Protection Law (PDPB), Thailand's Personal Data Protection Act (PDPA), Brazil's Lei Geral de Proteção de Dados Pessoais (LGPD) and China's Personal Information Protection Law (PIPL). These laws prevent firms from processing personal data, where the term "processing" encompasses a wide range of operations, including collecting, combining and storing personal data.

The main purpose of these laws is to protect users' "privacy". In fact, comprehensive reviews of privacy literature emphasize that there is no widely agreed-upon definition of privacy (Bleier, Goldfarb, and Tucker (2020), Martin and Murphy (2017), Norberg, Horne, and Horne (2007) and Wieringa et al. 2021). Westin (1967) defined privacy as "the ability of the individual to control the terms under which personal information is acquired and used." The GDPR effectively relies on this conceptualization of privacy, as its main provisions focus on users' control over their personal data. Herein, we adopt a similar perspective of the construct of privacy—with some extensions. For example, in line with a common approach in the popular media, we assume that a more extensive collection of data from consumers implies less privacy.

In restricting the processing of personal data, privacy laws affect online advertising and, thus, the different actors operating in the online advertising market. Though several studies have begun to explore these effects (e.g., Peukert et al. 2022; Schmitt, Miller, and Skiera 2022), researchers and policymakers have yet to obtain a comprehensive and precise understanding of the implications of privacy laws for the online advertising market. This lack of clarity is unfortunate because as regulations continue to be formulated or updated, it is crucial for regulators and societies at large to understand the trade-off between user privacy and the economic value that the online advertising industry derives from processing personal data through potentially privacy-infringing technologies. Likewise, firms in the online advertising industry need to understand the implications of stricter privacy requirements for their performance, so as to adjust to these requirements effectively. Finally, users also deserve to understand what happens with their data, and the consequences of such data usage, or restrictions thereof.

One important reason for the lack of clarity on the implications of privacy laws for advertising is that the online advertising market is difficult to understand. It is a high-tech industry that comprises several extensive networks with many actors, as we will illustrate in these pages (see, in particular, our illustration of the complexity of the industry in Section 2 and our empirical study in Section 8). From a technological perspective, these actors accomplish extraordinary feats, such as conducting billions of auctions with many participants each day to sell single ad impressions in less than 100 milliseconds, or displaying personalized ads to millions of users.

Because of the complex technologies used in online advertising, effective decision-making in this market requires combining a technological perspective (e.g., finding the best technology to track users) with a marketing perspective (e.g., finding the best users to target). With the launch of far-reaching privacy laws such as the GDPR, it is becoming increasingly important for actors in this industry to consider the legal perspective as well. The need to combine these three perspectives implies that professionals in the advertising field must possess some level of expertise in multiple domains. For example, lawyers in the advertising industry need to understand what "cookies" and "consent strings" are, and marketing managers and IT experts need to understand the meanings of legal terms such as "legitimate interest" or "identifiable individual".

Our vision for this book is, thus, to provide an accessible yet comprehensive synthesis of what is currently known about how privacy laws—particularly the GDPR—affect the online advertising market. To this end, we highlight the requirements stipulated in the GDPR that are most relevant to the advertising industry, and we further clarify the implications of these requirements for the key actors in this industry, as well as for users. In doing so, we aim to provide actors in this market (in particular advertisers, publishers and users), as well as regulators and society at large, with better tools to (i) assess the trade-off between the benefits and the costs of more privacy, (ii) understand problems in implementing the requirements of GDPR, and (iii) draw conclusions on how to deal with the stricter privacy requirements that come with privacy laws such as the GDPR.

The remainder of this book is organized as follows. Section 2 outlines how the online advertising industry operates. Section 3 provides a basic overview of tracking technologies, the ways in which publishers, advertisers, and other firms use them, and the implications of tracking for users. Section 4 elaborates on the contents of the GDPR, focusing on the obligations relevant to firms in the advertising industry. In Section 5, we discuss the GDPR requirement that affects the advertising industry most profoundly: the need to secure a legal basis for data processing, which, in practice, entails obtaining user permission for data processing for specific purposes—e.g., via consent management tools, discussed in Section 6. Section 7 provides a step-by-step description of the procedure that firms must undertake to obtain user permission for data processing, and it presents a framework developed by IAB Europe, Europe's industry association for digital marketing and advertising, to assist firms in accomplishing this process (the Transparency and Consent Framework; TCF). Section 8 provides an empirical assessment of the complexity that firms face in obtaining permission, as well as the complexity that users face in handling permission requests. Section 9 provides an outlook on future developments in the advertising industry and in the regulatory landscape with regard to the processing of users' personal data. Finally, Section 10 provides conclusions.

2

Overview of the Online Advertising Industry

2.1 Essential Actors: Advertisers, Publishers and Users

Online advertising is, in basic terms, a process in which an advertiser pays a publisher to present an ad to a user on the publisher's property (usually a website or an app). Thus, there are three essential actors in online advertising (in alphabetical order):

- the *advertiser*, who wishes to draw the user's interest to the advertiser's offerings;
- the *publisher*, who has some space to show ads and would like to "monetize the user" by selling those ad spaces to the advertiser;
- the *user*, who is primarily interested in the publisher's offering (e.g., the content of a news website) and is sometimes also interested in the ads displayed on the site.

Figure 1 outlines the business models of advertisers and publishers; the exchanges that occur among advertisers, publishers and users; and the (often implicit) agreements among them.

Figure 1: *Interplay among the Essential Actors of the Online Advertising Market*

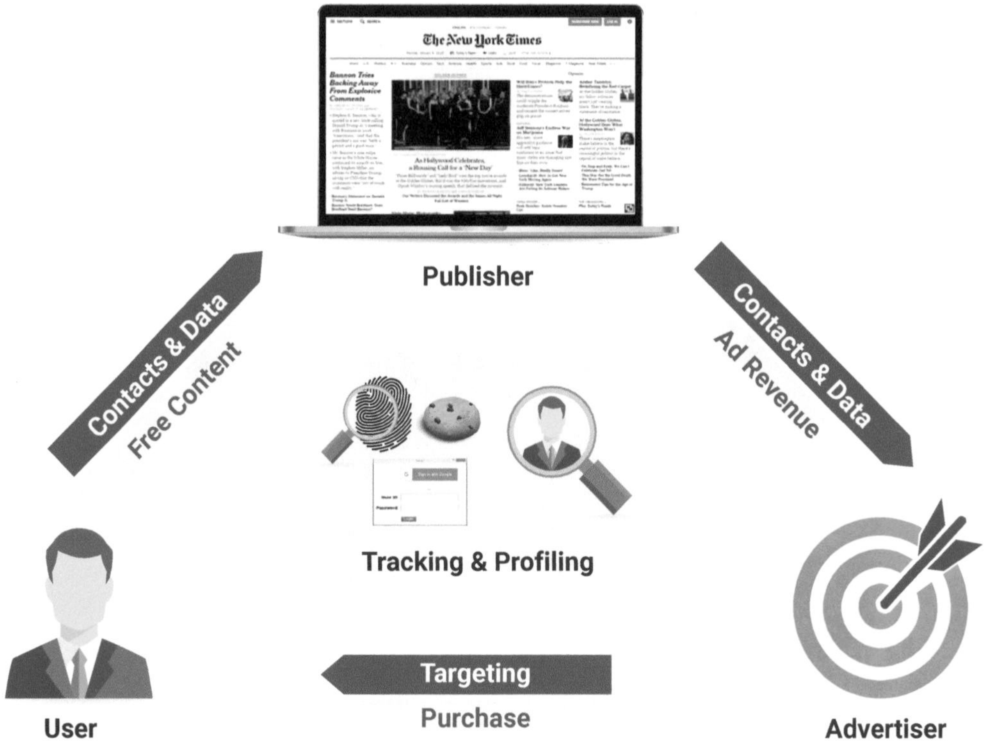

Many publishers offer users "free" access to their content—e.g., news—in exchange for the ability to collect data from these users, as well as to provide other actors, such as advertisers, with opportunities to contact the users. Thus, even when users ostensibly receive content without paying for it, they are still paying—not with money but with their data and willingness to view ads. Advertisers pay publishers for the opportunity to contact users and, to a lesser extent, pay for data about those users. Advertisers then proceed to display ads to users and, in cases in which relevant data are available, they may target certain users and even personalize ads to their preferences. Users, in turn, are expected to see those ads and, at least in some cases, to "purchase" the advertiser's offerings—where a purchase is broadly defined as a desired action that benefits the advertiser (including, for example, buying products, subscribing to an online newsletter, signing up for a test drive of a car, downloading a document, or donating).

At the heart of this interplay between the various actors is the tracking of users, which provides advertisers with two key capabilities. The first is the capacity to process data about users for profiling, which enables advertisers to better target ads to appropriate users, and thus to avoid wastage of ads. For example, an advertiser likely prefers to avoid sending a male user an ad for female hygiene products (and the other way around). The second is the capacity to recognize, at least to some extent, whether the ads are successful—which, in turn, enables the advertiser to determine whether it is worthwhile to continue spending money on a given publisher (and, ultimately, on the publisher's users). For example, if an ad served on a particular publisher does not receive any user reaction (as measured, e.g., by clicks on the ad), the advertiser might then conclude that, for the specific advertisement, the publisher does not attract the right audience, i.e., the right type of user. Alongside these benefits, however, user tracking raises privacy concerns, as elaborated in subsequent sections.

2.2 Scope and Types of Online Advertising

The online advertising industry is large and represents an essential part of the economy. Internet advertising revenues have grown consistently over recent years; in 2020, for example, the growth rate in the US was an impressive 12.2%, with revenues reaching $139.8b (IAB 2021). Advertisers spent 70% of all online advertising funds on advertising on mobile devices (including smartphones and tablets) and 30% on desktop platforms. Regarding ad format, the largest share of funds (42.2%, see Figure 2) is spent on search engine ads, i.e., ads delivered via search engines, notably Google. Display advertising (i.e., banner advertising) represents the second-largest share (31.5%), and video advertising, e.g., on YouTube, the third-largest share (18.7%). Other forms of online advertising (e.g., classified advertising, audio formats, lead generation ads) play a minor role.

The ad-selling market is highly concentrated; indeed, in 2020, the top 10 publishers realized 78.1% of all advertising revenues (IAB 2021). Google and Facebook are by far the two largest publishers in the Western world. The ad-buying marketing is far less concentrated, i.e., there are no advertisers that dominate the demand side in a manner comparable to Google and Facebook on the supply side.

Figure 2: *Size and Share of Different Formats of Online Advertising in the US (IAB 2021)*

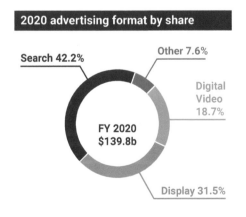

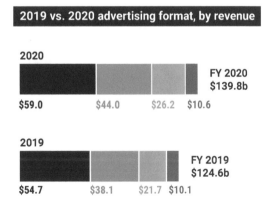

Figure 3 outlines the digital advertising spend per capita for selected European countries (IAB 2020). Advertising expenditures per internet user are, by far, highest in the UK (324.70€), followed by Norway (231.30€), Sweden (229.40€), Switzerland (212.40€) and Denmark (194.80€). In Germany, the average amount spent per Internet user is 113.40€.

Figure 3: *Digital Advertising Spend per Capita in 15 Countries (IAB 2020)*

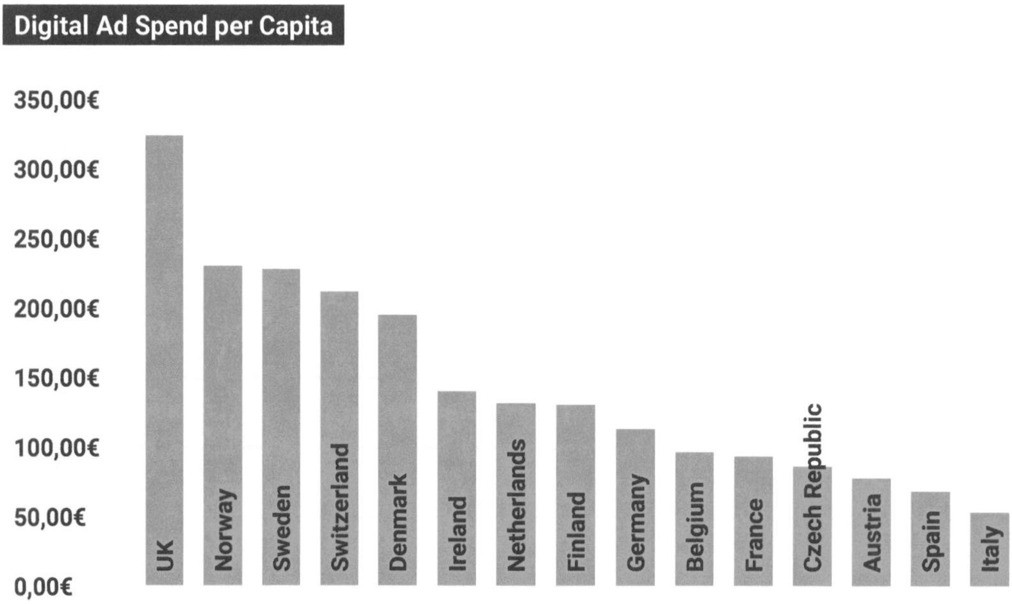

2.3 Real-Time Bidding as a Process of Selling Online Advertising

In this subsection, we describe a prominent process of selling online advertising, which we refer to as "real-time bidding" (RTB), and which is also referred to in the industry as "programmatic advertising", because advertisers and publishers use algorithms to buy and sell advertising (Kosorin 2016). The 2021 IAB report (IAB 2021) outlines that 88% of ads (excluding search) sell as programmatic advertising. This process constitutes a key source of concern for regulators and privacy advocates. For clarity of presentation, in what follows, our discussion focuses primarily on online display advertising (also referred to as banner advertising) but selling digital video ads shares many characteristics. Online display advertising is well known to most users and raises many privacy concerns because it often involves exchanging data between firms. It uses an auction-based system to sell ads, as search ads also do. Other forms of advertising, including traditional offline advertising such as TV and outdoor, gradually implement comparable systems.

Real-time bidding is a collective term for the technological infrastructure used to sell opportunities to display an ad in real-time and in a fully automated manner (Yuan, Wang, and Zhao 2013, Wang, Zhang, and Yuan 2017). In many cases, selling occurs via real-time auctions that run for less than 100 milliseconds (for reference, a blink of an eye takes 200-400 milliseconds). Ad exchanges (e.g., Xandr), marketplaces that connect advertisers and publishers, frequently serve as platforms for such real-time auctions (Cristal 2014, Kosorin 2016, Lee, Jalali, and Dasdan 2013, Information Commissioner's Office 2019; Ada, Abou Nabout, and McDonnell Feit 2022).

Figure 4 illustrates the automated auction process under real-time bidding. For convenience, we refer to a scenario in which an ad slot is being sold on a website, but the general process we describe is applicable to other online media that belong to a publisher and contain ad slots, such as apps. As shown in the figure, whenever a user visits a publisher's website with ad slots (1), the publisher sends an ad call to an ad exchange (2). This ad call is a request to run a real-time auction on the ad exchange and contains information about, for example, the properties of the ad slot (e.g., ad size) and a user ID, which we explain in more detail in Section 3.1. The ad exchange then sends a bid request to all advertisers on the ad exchange (3). Each interested advertiser submits a bid for displaying its ad to the user; the bid also includes the ad server's address with the ad (4). The ad exchange determines the price and the winner of the auction and forwards this information to the publisher (5). The publisher then asks the user's browser to load the ad from the ad server (6), and the ad is subsequently displayed to the user on the publisher's website (7).

Figure 4: *Illustration of the Auction Process in Real-Time Bidding (RTB)*

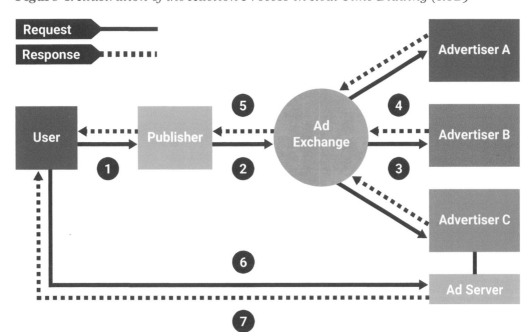

This description of the real-time auction process is a simplification, because it only captures essential steps (for more details, see Cristal 2014, Kosorin 2016, Trusov, Ma, and Jamal 2016 or Wang, Zhang, and Yuan 2017). It does not consider, for example, the specific requirements imposed by privacy laws such as the GDPR (which we will outline later in Section 6 when discussing the Transparency and Consent Framework (TCF)). In addition, it is important to acknowledge that there are many other actors that support the activities of advertisers and publishers (Luma Partners 2021). We describe these other actors in the following subsection.

2.4 Description of Other Actors

Figure 5 classifies the numerous actors in the online advertising industry into several main groups that we will not all cover here.

Figure 5: *Overview of Actors in the Online Advertising Industry (DisplayLUMAscape)*

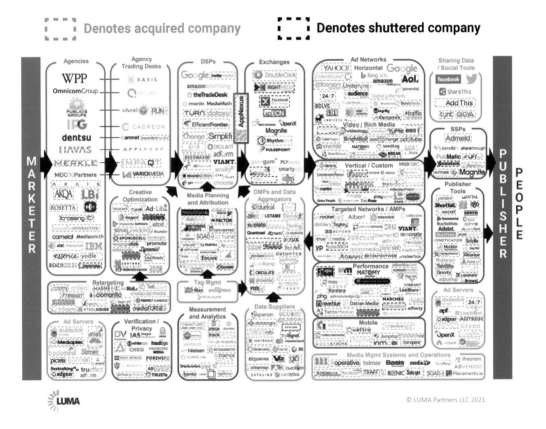

Note that Luma Partners (2021) refer in this figure to an advertiser as a "marketer" and to users as "people".

An ad exchange, as noted above, is a marketplace where the demand side, i.e., advertisers, and the supply side, i.e., publishers, meet to fill ad slots (offered by publishers) with ads (provided by advertisers). A demand-side platform (DSP) is a technology provider that supports the advertiser buying ad slots. A supply-side platform (SSP) provides technology to support the publisher selling its ad slots. An advertising agency helps the advertiser with the creation of the ad. An ad server is a web server (i.e., a computer) that stores advertising content (e.g., banner ads). It delivers that content to the publisher's ad slot and, thus, the user (in our setting, the user's browser).

Many additional actors exist that support the process of selling ad slots and delivering ads to those ad slots. Among them are data management platforms (DMPs), which provide data about the user (e.g., demographics or user interests), or verification providers that verify that an ad appears on the correct publisher. The advertiser and the publisher have to finance all actors. As a result, the price that the advertiser pays for an ad is often much higher than the amount that the publisher receives. Google, for example, outlines that its publishers received over 69% of the money that the advertiser paid (Hsiao 2020). The share of the money that the publisher receives goes further down if the seller and buying of ads involve more actors. For example, the Guardian reports that this share can drop to 30% (Pidgeon 2016).

Figure 6 provides a schematic illustration of how the various actors operate together to produce what the user ultimately views (in terms of both content and ads). In effect, when the user visits a publisher's website (e.g., a news website), two processes are initiated. The first process (marked in orange) delivers the website's primary content (in our example, news content). This content is available on the publisher's content server. The second process (marked in blue) is the process through which ads slots are sold and ads are delivered to the user. Our discussion focuses on the latter process; accordingly, in Figure 6, the process marked in orange is simplified and does not include other actors that may be involved in content delivery, such as measurement and analytics providers that track, for example, how often a user saw certain content and that help the publisher optimize its content.

Figure 6: *Delivery of Content and Ads from the User's Perspective when Visiting a Website*

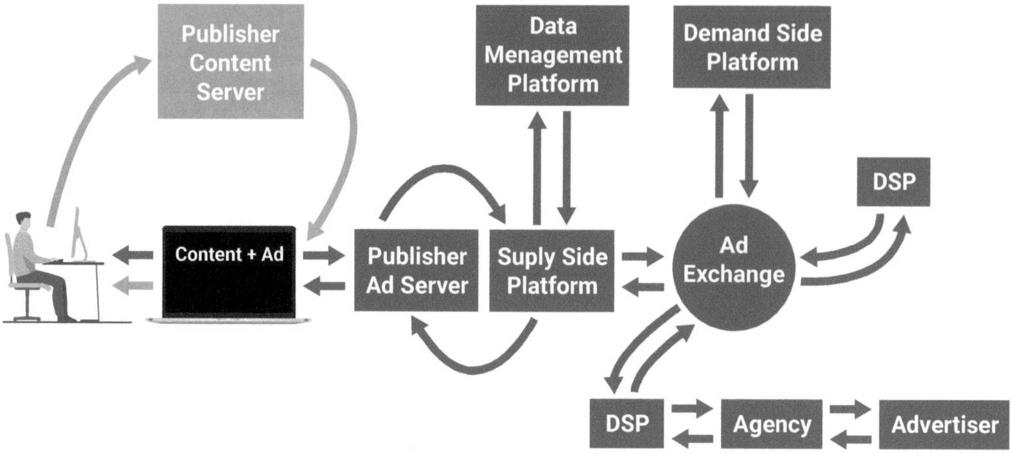

The process of selling ad slots and delivering ads involves the following steps. The publisher's ad server recognizes an available ad slot (usually even multiple ad slots) that the publisher would like to fill with an ad. The ad server approaches the supply-side platform (SSP) with a request to sell the ad slot on the ad exchange. The SSP sets up the auction on the ad exchange, and the ad exchange approaches the advertisers, usually via several demand-side platforms (DSPs), with a request for a quote for the ad slot, i.e., offering the opportunity to buy the opportunity to display an ad to the specific user. It is essential to understand that any data that the publisher reveals can spread to many other actors. That is a concern that Ryan (2018) raises. He outlines that it is technically feasible to share a wide range of information along the chain outlined in Figure 6. Such sharing raises privacy concerns. It is, however, less clear whether and how intensively sharing of personal data occurs.

2.5 Main Takeaways

The main takeaways from Section 2 are:

- The three main actors in the online advertising industry are advertisers, publishers, and users. Between each pair of actors, a transaction takes place—whether implicitly or explicitly agreed upon.
- 70% of online advertising occurs on mobile devices (including smartphones and tablets). The main advertising formats are search engine advertising, online display advertising and video advertising.

- Real-time bidding is the primary process through which the selling of display advertising occurs. Data sharing in real-time bidding is a source of privacy concerns.

- Many publishers rely on advertising to finance their content. They often do not charge users, but users then pay by providing publishers and advertisers (often implicitly) with data, as well as willingness to view ads.

- Selling and displaying online (display) advertising involves many different actors and requires sophisticated technologies. Indeed, the online advertising industry is effectively a high-tech industry.

3

User Tracking, Profiling, and Targeting in Online Advertising

3.1 Description of User Tracking Technologies

In simple terms, user tracking describes the practice of collecting data about users over time (Kraft, Miller, and Skiera 2022). User tracking gathers data that reveal insights into various characteristics of the user, such as the user's demographics (e.g., female), interests (e.g., high interest in fashion), brand preferences (e.g., Adidas), or purchase intentions (e.g., being in the market for sports shoes). Publishers and advertisers can use such tracking of a user over time to generate a profile for the user to target him or her with unique advertising or content.

Numerous technologies exist for user tracking; in what follows, we discuss some of the most important ones. For clarity of presentation, in our discussion, we classify the various technologies along two main dimensions:

- The number of *devices* on which the user is tracked: just one device (i.e., single-device tracking) versus multiple devices (i.e., cross-device tracking);
- The number of *websites* on which the user is tracked: a single publisher's website (i.e., first-party website) versus multiple websites (i.e., third-party websites).

Figure 7 presents this classification.

Figure 7: *Categorization of User Tracking Technologies*

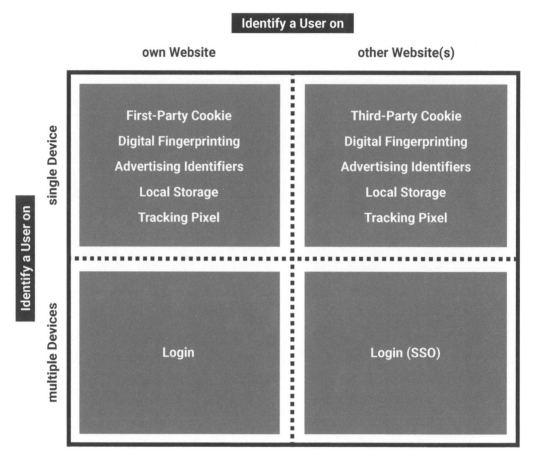

3.1.1 Single-Device User Tracking

Single-device user tracking technologies track a user only on one specific device (e.g., on a desktop computer, mobile phone, or tablet). Moreover, in most cases, single-device user tracking technologies only track a user within one browser (e.g., Google Chrome) on that device. The most popular single-device tracking technologies are first- and third-party cookies. Additional technologies include digital fingerprinting, advertising identifiers, local storage, and tracking pixels.

3.1.1.1 Cookies

A cookie (also referred to as an "HTTP cookie", Internet cookie, or browser cookie) is, in simplified terms, a small piece of data sent from a publisher's or advertiser's server (i.e., a website) to a user's browser and stored on the user's device (Cristal 2014). A cookie usually contains a unique number called a "Cookie-ID" that identifies the user, e.g.,

"177'239'342'526'456'932". Each cookie also has an expiration date, which is the date on which the browser will automatically delete the cookie. Every time a user accesses the website (or one of the websites) to which the cookie belongs (see below for further details on how different types of cookies track users across one or multiple websites), the website reads the cookie and stores its Cookie-ID, alongside information about the user's behavior during the visit. In most cases, this information is stored on the server of the firm (i.e., the computer of the publisher or advertiser) that created the cookie.

The cookie's unique identifier enables the firm to link several visits of the user together. Cookies are stored in the user's browser storage (meaning that a particular cookie can typically only link a user's visits on a single browser). All major browsers enable users to prevent cookies or to delete cookies. If the user deletes a cookie and, thus, the associated Cookie-ID, the firm can no longer re-identify the user on the next visit to the website. Instead, the firm will consider the user to be a new user and create a new cookie. There is no connection between the new and the old Cookie-ID and the stored data associated with the two Cookie-IDs.

There are three types of cookies, respectively data: first-party cookies, second-party cookies and third-party cookies. First-party cookies are installed by the website that the user is visiting, e.g., a publisher such as the *New York Times*. So, all data collected by *New York Times* on its website is first-party data. A simple test of whether a cookie is a first-party cookie is whether the cookie comes from the domain whose name appears in the user's browser window. A user can easily look up the installed cookies in their browser. For example, in Google Chrome a user could type in the browser space "chrome://settings/siteData" instead of typing the website's URL they want to visit to see her cookies.

A second-party cookie is a cookie set by another website that belongs to the same owner. So, a publisher's second-party data refers to data received from the property (e.g., a website or an app) of a publisher that belongs to the same owner. For example, Meta's Social Network's second-party data is the data that the social network, Facebook, receives from other properties of the Meta conglomerate, such as Instagram, Oculus, or WhatsApp (Kraft, Miller, and Skiera 2022).

A third-party cookie, in turn, is installed by a website that does not belong to the publisher that the user is visiting, e.g., a third-party ad server that is, for example, owned by a large advertising agency such as Havas. Third-party cookies can track a user across multiple websites. Third-party cookies can be placed in a user's cookie storage within the user's browser via an ad that an advertiser displays on a publisher's website. Specifically, because the user's browser loads the ad's content from the advertiser's server, the advertiser's server can store a third-party cookie on the user's device.

So, a publisher's third-party data refers to data received from the property of another publisher that does not belong to the same owner and, thus, is a third party. For example,

Meta's Social Network's third-party data is data that Facebook receives from third-party websites via the Facebook Share Button (among others).

Our distinction into first-party and second-party cookies, respectively data, is hardly made. Instead, both types are treated as first-party cookies, respectively data. This treatment is unfortunate because it hides an advantage that conglomerates such as Google or Facebook have. They can obtain consent only once and then bundle the information collected on all of their properties. This ability is in contrast to a situation in which each property belonged to a different owner. For example, Meta combines data from Facebook, Instagram, WhatsApp and Oculus because they all belong to Facebook, despite these firms being all separate legal entities. Ryan (2020) refers to this opportunity as "internal data free-for-all".

Other forms of cookies exist. Some of these cookies are designed with the aim of better identifying users or making the deletion of cookies more difficult. A supercookie (also called evercookie or zombie cookie), for example, is a cookie that is stored in multiple storages on a user's device. The basic idea of a supercookie is that the user does not know where all cookie instances are stored. Consequently, if the user deletes the cookie in several but not all places, then the cookie instances in the remaining places can simply re-create the cookie in the places from which it was deleted. As a result, a supercookie is difficult to delete, enhancing the firm's ability to track the user.

The online advertising industry has a strong interest in knowing which cookies belong to the same user. However, the fact that different (first- or third-party) cookies use different identifiers makes it very difficult for different websites to identify a single user. For example, the Cookie-ID A-001 on website A and the Cookie-ID B-007 on website B might belong to the same user, but an advertiser bidding to display ads on the two websites has no straightforward way of knowing this. To help alleviate this problem, technologies such as cookie syncing facilitate the exchange of Cookie-IDs that belong to cookies of different websites.

Cookie syncing allows an advertiser to link the user's third-party Cookie-ID (e.g., Cookie-ID A-001 to the Cookie-IDs of (first- or third-party) cookies sent by other publishers or advertisers (e.g., Cookie-ID B-007). This process enables the advertiser to incorporate the user data associated with the various Cookie-IDs beyond her own Cookie-ID. The process of cookie syncing is usually a part of data-buying and -sharing agreements between different actors in the online advertising industry such as publishers and advertisers, but also ad networks, demand-side platforms (DSPs), data management platforms, ad exchanges, supply-side platforms (SSPs), and various other data providers. Cookie syncing benefits advertisers and publishers by increasing the amount of data available regarding each user, across different platforms, thereby improving the capacity to target users with online advertisements.

3.1.1.2 Digital Fingerprinting

Digital fingerprinting involves gathering information about a user's device, and exploiting this information to identify the user. Fingerprinting can be either passive or active. Passive fingerprinting involves gathering information about the configuration of a user's device. Such a configuration has many attributes—e.g., CPU type, computer clock skew, display settings, scripts that are used, browser and operating system information, IP address, or language settings—and a passive fingerprint is essentially a string that contains all of this information. For example, the string "intel:00:00:01:chrome:windows" would be a passive fingerprint that includes CPU type, computer clock skew, browser, and operating system. Because there are so many different ways to configure a device, the specific combination that a particular user has is likely to be unique, thereby providing a means of identifying the user. Still, there is no guarantee that there are no other devices with the same combination of these attributes. Active fingerprints, in turn, are digital fingerprints that include information that is guaranteed to be unique to the user's device (e.g., the media access control (MAC) address provided by the chipmaker). To get an active and thus unique fingerprint, the publisher or the advertiser interested in tracking the user installs executable code on the user's device and reads its MAC (or another unique serial number).

A publisher can use active or passive fingerprinting to track a user on its first-party website. Advertisers can use active or passive fingerprinting to follow a user on third-party websites. Advertisers can obtain the information required to generate a fingerprint by displaying an ad on the publisher's website. When the user accesses the publisher's website, the user's browser loads the website's content from the publisher's server, and it loads the content of the ad from the advertiser's server (see Figure 6). When the user's browser accesses the advertiser's server to display the ad, the advertiser's server can generate the digital fingerprint. In addition to tracking a user on a third-party website, advertisers (such as Adidas) can also track a user on their own (first-party) websites (e.g., Adidas.com) using active or passive fingerprinting.

Behavioral biometric features, namely dynamics that occur when typing, moving, and clicking the mouse, or touching a touch screen, can provide further information to improve active digital fingerprinting and, hence, user identification.

3.1.1.3 Advertising Identifiers

Another single-device user tracking technology used on mobile devices (so-called mobile apps) relies on advertising identifiers, called mobile ad IDs (MAIDs). An advertising identifier is a string of hexadecimal digits assigned to a given device by the device's operating system, e.g., Apple's iOS or Google's Android. Apple's MAID is called Identifier for Advertisers (IDFA), and Google's MAID is called Google Advertising Identifier (GAID).

The identifiers are device-specific. Thus, all ad networks in all apps running on the same device will get the same ID. In mobile browsers, the advertising IDs are not usable. Advertising identifiers are nowadays also used for other connected devices such as for example voice assistants, connected television (CTV), or over-the-top (OTT) devices.

3.1.1.4 Local Storage

Local storage–based tracking relies on the possibility to store data in the so-called local storage of the user's browser. Publishers and advertisers can use the local storage to save text-based information such as a unique user ID and other information to track a user's online behavior. The browser's local storage is a place to store items that are usually not passed back and forth constantly to publishers' or advertisers' servers. Also, first- and third-party websites can access and use local storage to identify a user. The local storage is usually part of the user's browser and allows publishers and advertisers to save data with up to 5 MB in the user's browser. There is no expiration date for the data stored. Thus, data items within the local storage are available until the website or the user deletes them. One downside of local storage is that it is not very secure. Therefore, unencrypted private or personal information should not be stored in the local storage.

3.1.1.5 Tracking Pixel

A tracking pixel (also called a pixel tag, web beacon, action tag, or clear GIF) is a piece of code that creates a 1×1 pixel; this code is embedded either in the HTML code of a publisher's website—thereby allowing the publisher to track users on its website—or in the HTML code of an ad displayed on the publisher's website—thereby enabling the advertiser to track the user on the website. Beyond HTML, tracking pixels can also be integrated in JavaScript or an iFrame. When a user visits a website containing a tracking pixel, the browser loads the pixel from the server of the firm (publisher or advertiser) that created the pixel. This loading enables the firm to access the user's browser. A tracking pixel allows a firm to track a user because the pixel is loaded from an external URL so that this external URL, respectively the firm behind this URS, can track the user.

Tracking pixels are invisible to the user and do not store on a user's computing device. Accordingly, without inspecting a website's underlying HTML code, users cannot know whether they are being tracked by a pixel. Tracking pixels can also document how far a user scrolls down a page.

3.1.2 Cross-Device User Tracking

Cross-device user tracking technologies enable a user's online behavior to be tracked across multiple devices. One means by which firms accomplish cross-device user tracking is by asking a user to log in to a personal account from any device connected to the internet. For example, if a user uses multiple devices—e.g., her mobile phone, her laptop, and her desktop computer—to access a particular website (e.g., her favorite news website, e-mail service, or social networking site), the website can easily and accurately track her activities across all those devices (and across multiple browsers within those devices) on the basis of her login. As will be elaborated in what follows, a login can facilitate cross-device tracking not only on first-party websites but also on third-party websites.

3.1.2.1 Cross-Device User Tracking on a First-Party Website

Technically, a user login on a first-party website is accomplished using a single-device user tracking technology such as a cookie. Suppose a user accesses a website through a web browser on her device. In that case, the website can implement the user login by placing a cookie on the device to remember the user in the future. In this case, the cookie enables a so-called automatic login so that the user does not have to reenter her password every time she visits the website. Such a login identifies a user across multiple visits to the same website.

However, firms also use a cookie to keep a user logged in while the user browses multiple webpages during a single visit to a website. Other devices may allow similar tracking tools to enable the website to recognize the device in the future, such as a device-specific advertising identifier on smartphones. The user's data is then typically stored on the server of the website that provides the login to the user.

3.1.2.2 Cross-Device User Tracking on a Third-Party Website

Another form of user login that tracks the user across multiple third-party websites is the single sign-on (SSO). Here the user login is forwarded by the provider of the user login to other websites. From the user's perspective, only one login exists. With this user login, the user can quickly log in to all websites that support the SSO. Examples of SSO providers are Facebook, Google, and the German provider netID. NetID was established in March 2018 as a foundation to offer an independent alternative to the SSO offerings of Google and Facebook (see also Section 9.2).

3.1.3 Comparison of User Tracking Technologies

Table 1 presents a comparison of the user tracking technologies discussed in the previous subsections. We compare the various technologies by the following six criteria:

- **User Identification:** Describes whether a user tracking technology identifies a user on a first-party website (e.g., the publisher's website) or third-party website (e.g., other publishers' websites), and whether a user tracking technology identifies a user on a single device (e.g., only on a desktop computer) or on multiple devices (e.g., on a desktop computer and a mobile phone).

- **Storage of User Identifier:** Describes whether a user tracking technology stores a user's identifier (e.g., a cookie) on the user's side (i.e., the user's client, for example, a user's browser) or on the firm's side (i.e., the firm's server).

- **Storage of Information on User:** Describes whether a user tracking trechnology stores a user"s information on the user's side (i.e., the user's client, for example, a user's browser) or on the firm's side (i.e., the firm's server).

- **Expiration of User Identifier:** Describes whether a user identifier (e.g., a cookie) expires after some pre-defined date (e.g., after one year of setting the user identifier).

- **Deletability of User Identifier and Information on User:** Describes whether the user can delete the user's identifier (e.g., a cookie) or the information about the user (e.g., by deleting the user's browser cache).

- **Alteration of User Identifier:** Describes whether a user can alter the user identifier, for example, by changing the user's browser configuration (e.g., choosing a different browser font or language) or by changing the user's login information (e.g., the user's email address).

Table 1 illustrates that the most favorable user tracking technology from a firm's perspective is the SSO. An SSO allows a firm to track a user on its own (first-party) website and on other (third-party) websites, as well as across multiple devices (e.g., on the user's desktop and mobile device). Because the user's identifier and information are stored on the firm's side (i.e., the firm's server), a firm has more control over the identifier and the data collected on a specific user in the past. In addition, the SSO does not expire (unlike cookies, for example). However, the user can delete or alter the SSO, preventing a firm from connecting existing data to new data from the same user.

Despite their advantages, SSOs are difficult for a firm to obtain, as not all firms provide users with sufficient value to justify their signing up for an SSO. In such a case, firms have to rely on other tracking technologies such as cookies, which may also explain cookies' enduring popularity as a user tracking technology despite their disadvantages.

Table 1: *Comparison of Most Important User Tracking Technologies*

		User Tracking Technology								
		First-Party Cookie	Second-Party Cookie	Third-Party Cookie	Digital Fingerprinting	Advertising Identifiers	Local Storage	Tracking Pixel	Login	Single-Sign-On (SSO)
User Identification	First-party Website (Own Website)	✓			✓	✓	✓	✓		✓
	Second-party Website (Other Website with the same Owner)		✓		✓	✓	✓	✓		✓
	Third-party Website (Other Website with different Owner)			✓	✓	✓	✓	✓		✓
	Single Device	✓	✓	✓	✓	✓	✓		✓	✓
	Multiple Devices								✓	✓
Storage of User Identifier	User-side (Client)	✓	✓	✓		✓	✓	✓		
	Firm-side (Server)	✓	✓	✓	✓				✓	✓
Storage of Information on User	User-side (Client)	✓	✓	✓		✓	✓	✓		
	Firm-side (Server)	✓	✓	✓	✓	✓	✓		✓	✓
Expiration of User Identifier		✓	✓	✓						
Deletability (by User)	Deletability of User Identifier	✓	✓	✓		✓	✓			
	Deletability of Information on User	✓	✓	✓			✓			
User Can Alter User Identifier					✓	✓			✓	✓

3.2 Importance of Tracking, Profiling, and Targeting for the Online Advertising Industry

In this subsection, we discuss the practical applications of the technologies discussed above, from advertisers' and publishers' perspectives. Following Kraft, Miller, and Skiera (2022), we distinguish between tracking, profiling, and targeting (Figure 8). Loosely speaking, as noted above, tracking refers to collecting data about users over time (which might include personal data). Profiling involves identifying the data that are valuable for the firm, and using these data to create information about individual users (e.g., characterizing users according to demographic information such as age and gender). This step can enable a firm to distinguish between users that it views as more valuable versus less valuable. Finally, targeting refers to using these profiles to treat some users differently from others. For advertisers, targeting involves selecting profiles of users who are likely to be suitable audiences for a specific ad (e.g., women with kids), or conversely, selecting ads that are likely to be suitable for a specific user. For a publisher, targeting generally involves presenting users with content (e.g., news content for a news publisher) that suits their interests.

Figure 8: *Relationship between Tracking, Profiling and Targeting for Online Advertising*

We note that herein, we focus on targeting users on the basis of data that have been collected about them through tracking technologies; this form of targeting is referred to as "behavioral targeting" in Figure 9. It contains "retargeting", also referred to as "remarketing" or "behavioral retargeting" (Lambrecht and Tucker 2013; Bleier and Eisenbeiss 2015; Sahni, Narayanan, and Kalyanam 2019). A typical setting for retargeting is an online shop where a user puts a product into a shopping basket but does not purchase it. The online shop can now inform a retargeting provider such as Criteo about this behavior. The retargeting provider then puts up ads of the online shop and the abandoned product on many other websites. So, the user suddenly observes an ad about the specific product on another website (e.g., an online newspaper) even if this website is unrelated to the online shop (Miller and Skiera 2022).

Figure 9 outlines that "contextual targeting" is the other major form of targeting in online advertising. It uses the context in which the user appears (e.g., viewing a news forum on investment advice) to draw conclusions about the user's interests and the ads that are likely to be relevant for her. For example, a user reading an article about investment advice might be interested in financial products.

Figure 9: *Forms of Targeting in Online Advertising*

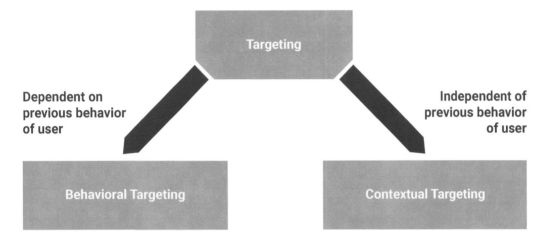

3.2.1 Importance for Advertisers

The capacity to accurately target users benefits advertisers in enabling them to avoid wastage, i.e., displaying ads to irrelevant users (users who are unlikely to wish to purchase the advertised products). For example, all else being equal, if an advertiser decreases wastage from 90% to 50%, then for any 10 users viewing the ad, the number of relevant users viewing the ad is expected to increase from 1 to 5. Advertisers are willing to pay for such a decrease in wastage: In our example, since the advertiser becomes five times more likely to reach a relevant user, she might be willing to pay five times more for the ad.

A common prerequisite for being willing to pay more for an ad is the ability to measure the success of an ad, and thereby to confirm that the ad is indeed reaching a relevant audience (in our example, this would mean confirming that the number of relevant users has increased from 1 to 5). Many success measures exist, with the most common being the following:

- users' probability of clicking on the ad, referred to as the "click-through rate" (i.e., the number of clicks divided by the number of impressions of the ad);
- users' probability of converting, referred to as the "conversion rate" (i.e., the number of conversions divided by the number of clicks on the ad); in many cases, a

conversion is defined as a purchase, but the term can also refer to a wide range of other actions that benefit the advertiser, such as subscribing to an online newsletter or signing up for a product demo;

- the product of the click-through rate and the conversion rate.

Advertisers' use of the success metrics above is not contingent on user tracking and profiling. That is, advertisers can use these metrics to compare the success rates of different ads, or of the same ad across different contexts—even without possessing knowledge of the specific behavior of individual users. Consider, for example, an advertiser who displays two ads for the same product, ad X and ad Y. If the advertiser observes that 50% of users who viewed ad X clicked on it, whereas 0% of users who viewed ad Y clicked on it, then she can determine that ad X was more successful than ad Y, even without knowing which specific users clicked on each ad.

Yet, information about individual behavior—obtained through the tracking technologies discussed above—enables the advertiser to analyze ad success on a more granular level. Going back to our example, let us assume that the advertiser can observe that ad X was viewed by user A—a male—and by user B—a female, and that user A clicked on the ad, whereas user B did not. In turn, ad Y was viewed by users C and D—both female—neither of whom clicked on the ad. This information might suggest to the advertiser that females are a less relevant audience for the advertised product, and that ad X was only more successful than ad Y because it was also shown to males.

The more detailed the information at the advertiser's disposal, the greater the capacity of the advertiser to link users' characteristics—e.g., demographics and interests such as being female and interested in running shoes —to their reactions towards the ad (e.g., their likelihood of clicking the ad). After establishing these links, the advertiser can derive the characteristics of users who are most likely to click, and subsequently target those users, i.e., ensure that ads are displayed only to them. For example, on the basis of user responses, an advertiser selling a protein shake may determine that its target audience is male users between the ages of 30 and 40 who are interested in sports. The advertiser can then ensure that she displays her ad only to users whose profiles match those characteristics. However, it is important to note that though user profiles may contain an enormous amount of information, this information is not always accurate or consistent (Neumann, Tucker, and Whitfield 2019; Kraft, Miller, and Skiera 2022). Erroneous profiles decrease advertisers' success with targeted ads and, thus, their willingness to pay for ads.

In addition to facilitating user targeting, tracking can enable advertisers to ensure that the same user is not exposed to the same ad too many times. Limitation of exposure can be achieved either through "frequency capping", i.e., limiting the number of times a user sees a particular ad, or through "recency capping", i.e., making sure that a minimum amount of time has elapsed since the user last saw the ad. Such capping could save the advertiser money and might also avoid annoying the user too much with the ad.

Finally, tracking enables the advertiser to conduct attribution modeling. It determines how much value each of several actions (also referred to as events or touchpoints) contributes to the desired outcome. Suppose, for example, that the user clicked on two ads and then purchased a product. The question is then whether both ads contributed equally to that purchase (so an attribution of 50% each) or not.

3.2.2 Importance for Publishers

Publishers also have an interest in tracking, profiling, and targeting. First, a publisher may offer a wide range of content, with different levels of appeal for each user. In these cases, the publisher may want to present each user with the content that is most suited to the user's interests. For example, a news website could prioritize displaying news about the user's favorite sports team or show the weather forecast for the particular area where the user lives. Profiling users can enable publishers to personalize their content in this manner.

Second, a publisher can track users to observe what they are doing on the website, and then use this knowledge for various purposes—such as improving the website. For example, user behavior might lead a publisher to make changes to the user interface (e.g., the publisher observes that users often leave the website on a particular page and then realizes that links were missing from the page), to the content of the website (e.g., by recognizing that certain topics of news articles are more attractive than others) or the presentation of the content (e.g., more pictures versus more text and vice versa). The improved website could then attract more users.

Third, user tracking enables publishers to document their websites' reach. While it is possible to measure a website's overall number of page impressions without tracking individual users, tracking is necessary in order to measure the number of unique (or different) users who visit a website—for the simple reason that such measurement requires observing whether a given user has visited the website before.

Advertisers often prefer publishers with an extensive reach. Accordingly, publishers are interested in reporting a high reach, and advertisers fear that publishers might over-report their reach. To avoid a lack of trust, publishers often ask a (trusted) third party to conduct the measurement, such as AGOF in Germany, which relies on information provided by INFOnline. AGOF also provides examples of their reports on their website (e.g., at www.agof.de/studien/daily-digital-facts/monatsberichte/, however, only in German).

The fourth benefit of tracking relates to the fact that the price that a publisher realizes from an ad impression is a function of the advertiser's willingness to pay (WTP) to display an ad to a particular user on the publisher's website. As discussed above, advertisers value the capacity to target specific users; thus, information that the publisher obtains about the user from tracking can, in theory, increase or decrease ad prices (e.g., Board 2009, Chen and Stallaert 2014, Levin and Milgrom 2010).

The following example illustrates how information gathered about a user can influence the ad prices that a publisher commands. Suppose there are two advertisers: Advertiser A, a producer of sports cars, and advertiser B, a producer of SUVs. Both advertisers prefer to target male users over female users. The advertisers are informed that an ad impression is available on a car review website. If the advertisers are informed that the user who will view the ad impression is male—as opposed to being provided with no information about the user's gender—their WTP may increase, leading to higher bids in the auction. As a result, the final price that the publisher receives for this impression can increase.

Yet, the influence of individual information on ad prices is not always straightforward. Suppose that, in addition, to determining that the user is male, the publisher has also determined that the user is interested in sports cars. This information might increase the WTP of advertiser A even more—but the WTP of advertiser B could decrease. In this case, the auction could lead to a *lower* price than in the situation where both advertisers only had information about the user's gender. Thus, theoretically, information about a user can increase or decrease ad prices. Empirical evidence suggests, however, that, on average, more information leads to higher ad prices (Johnson, Shriver, and Du 2020; Laub, Miller, Skiera 2021).

3.3 Implications for Users

There is little doubt that tracking, profiling and targeting benefit advertisers and publishers. It is, however, much more challenging to evaluate how users are affected by such tracking. In particular, users face a trade-off between certain benefits—such as utility from a more personalized browsing experience—and drawbacks, particularly a loss in privacy. In what follows, we elaborate on these benefits and drawbacks.

3.3.1 Personalization of Content

Personalization of content on publishers' websites—such as news feeds on social networks or product recommendations on online shopping or streaming platforms—can increase users' utility by providing them with experiences more directly related to their interests (Celis et al. 2019). It is important to acknowledge, however, that in providing personalized content, a publisher may seek to enhance not only the user's utility but also its own profit. Though these two perspectives may be aligned—because it is hard to make a profit by exposing a user to products or content that she is not interested in—they can still differ. For example, if product A provides slightly more utility to a user than product B, but the firm makes much more profit on product B, the firm is tempted to recommend product B.

Content personalization may also have certain disadvantages from the user's perspective. because an algorithmic recommendation can result in a "filter bubble", also referred to as an "echo chamber". In a filter bubble, a user is exposed only to content that is aligned with the user's own cultural background or ideology—a situation that is, at least in the long-run, in the interest of neither the user nor society. Furthermore, personalized content also discloses the preferences of the user, which the user might not appreciate.

3.3.2 Personalization of Ads

In addition to seeking to persuade users, advertising serves an informative function—for example, making users aware of products they may wish to purchase. Consequently, personalized (targeted) advertising may benefit users in providing them with information that is relevant to them, thereby helping them make better purchase decisions (for additional information on how users benefit from personalized ads, see a review by Boerman, Kruikemeier, and Borgesius 2017).

Personalized advertising can also benefit users in more indirect ways. The most obvious is that better targeting of ads enables the publisher to command higher prices for ads—and this revenue may enable the publisher to provide more content for "free", i.e., without charging a fee to users. Notably, as discussed in Section 2.1, such content is not actually "free", as users "pay" for it with their data and with the attention they devote to ads. Still, some users (e.g., those with little income) may prefer this mode of payment instead of paying with actual money.

3.3.3 Privacy

From the user's perspective, the major drawback of tracking is a violation of privacy. In general, surveys consistently suggest that users are uncomfortable with the idea of firms tracking their behavior over time and building up profiles. For example, a survey in 2019 showed that 79% of users worldwide are concerned about how firms use their data (Pew Research Center 2019). In another survey, 40% of users indicated feeling they have no control over their data (Presthus and Sørum 2018), partly due to an inability to oversee which data firms collect.

These reports notwithstanding, it is complex to evaluate users' actual preferences with regard to their privacy, because there is a significant disparity between users' stated preferences concerning privacy and the actual steps they take to protect it. This disparity is referred to as the "privacy paradox" (Aguirre et al. 2015, Norberg, Horne, and Horne 2007, Beke, Eggers, and Verhoef 2018). Usually, stated preferences reflect a desire for high privacy levels, whereas revealed preferences reflect an acceptance of substantially lower levels. For example, Gross and Acquisti (2005) scraped users' real-world social media privacy settings and found that few (1.2%) had altered permissive default settings. Athey, Catalini, and Tucker (2017) also documented a large gap between stated and revealed preferences for privacy.

Regardless of what users actually prefer, and as we will see below, regulators have concluded that a user's loss of privacy outweighs the potential benefits that come with better personalization of content and ads.

3.4 Main Takeaways

The main takeaways from Section 3 are:

- Cookies are a popular tracking technology, but they only track a user's behavior on one device and in one browser. Furthermore, users can easily delete cookies or prevent that firms set cookies.

- Single-Sign-On (SSO) is the most favorable user tracking technology from a firm's perspective. However, not all firms provide users with sufficient value to justify signing up for an SSO service. This shortcoming of SSOs may explain the enduring popularity of other tracking technologies, such as cookies.

- Advertisers and publishers benefit from tracking, profiling, and the resulting ability to target users with personalized content or ads. Tracking also enables advertisers to measure the success of advertising.

- It is challenging to evaluate whether users benefit from tracking, profiling and targeting. It requires trading-off between certain benefits—such as utility from a more personalized browsing experience—and drawbacks, particularly a loss in privacy.

- Measuring users' preference for privacy is tricky, because most users say that privacy is important—but their actions reveal a far more lenient stance toward privacy, a phenomenon called the "privacy paradox".

4

Personal Data Processing under the GDPR

4.1 Aim and Scope of the GDPR

The General Data Protection Regulation (GDPR) became effective in all member states of the European Union on May 25, 2018. The regulation aims to increase consumer privacy by (i) strengthening consumers' control over their personal data (see Section 4.2 for the GDPR's precise definition of personal data); and (ii) harmonizing EU member states' existing national privacy laws via one regulation for all EU member states. The GDPR achieves these aims both by defining users' rights with regard to their personal data (see Section 4.3) and by imposing obligations on firms that process such data (see Section 4.4). As elaborated in what follows, the GDPR defines the concept of personal data processing rather broadly—encompassing the collection of personal data, as well as the use and ultimate deletion of such data.

Unlike previous EU privacy laws, which only affected European firms, the GDPR applies not only to EU firms but also to firms outside the EU that process EU citizens' personal data. The only case in which the GDPR treats European firms and non-European firms differently is with regard to the processing of personal data of non-EU citizens; in these cases, the GDPR applies to European firms but not to non-European firms, as outlined in Table 2.

Table 2: *Applicability of the GDPR for EU and non-EU Firms Processing Personal Data of EU and non-EU Citizens*

	EU Citizen	Non-EU Citizen
EU Firm	Applicable	Applicable
Non-EU Firm	Applicable	Non-Applicable

4.2 Definition of Personal Data

The GDPR defines personal data as follows (Article 4):

> *[…] any information relating to an identified or identifiable natural person ('data subject'); an identifiable natural person is one who can be identified, directly or indirectly, in particular by reference to an identifier such as a name, an identification number, location data, an online identifier or to one or more factors specific to the physical, physiological, genetic, mental, economic, cultural or social identity of that natural person.*

According to this definition, and in contrast to prior regulations, which only considered information that directly identifies a consumer (e.g., name, address, birth date, or social security number) as personal data, the GDPR considers personal data to include any information that directly or indirectly identifies a user (Bleier, Goldfarb, Tucker 2020). Information that can indirectly identify a user includes online identifiers such as cookies and digital fingerprints. Therefore, firms that adopt such tracking techniques have to comply with the GDPR.

The GDPR strictly differentiates between pseudonymous data, to which the GDPR applies, and anonymous data, to which the GDPR does not apply. Personal data are considered pseudonymous if they do not directly identify a user but can be used to identify a user indirectly. For example, a customer number (e.g., "123456789") does not, in itself, directly identify a user. However, when combined with information relating the customer number to an individual user (e.g., "123456789" represents user "X"), the customer number is considered pseudonymous data. Personal data are only considered anonymized if they do not identify a user at all (e.g., it is unknown which user the customer number

"123456789" represents). Thus, firms that collect data from consumers and seek to avoid the GDPR cannot suffice with pseudonymizing user information but rather must anonymize it, which may be impractical and costly.

4.3 User Rights with Regard to Personal Data Processing

The GDPR provides users with eight rights related to the processing of their personal data. In what follows, and as summarized in Table 3, we classify these rights into three categories: rights that enable users to *understand* the processing of their personal data (Section 4.3.1); to *change* the processing of their personal data processing (Section 4.3.2), and to *restrict* the processing of their personal data (Section 4.3.3).

Table 3: *Overview of User Rights and Their Aims under the GDPR*

Aims of Rights	Rights
Understand the personal data processing	Right to Information
	Right to Access
Change the personal data processing	Right to Rectification
	Right to Erasure
	Right to Data Portability
Restrict the personal data processing	Right to Restriction of Processing
	Right to Object
	Right to Avoid Automated Decision Making

4.3.1 Rights Enabling Users to Understand the Processing of Their Personal Data

The "Right to Information" states that a user has a claim to information about any firm that processes the user's personal data and about the firm's personal data–processing activities. Such information includes the contact details of the firm, which types of personal data the firm processes, and the rationale behind the processing. For example, if a user shops on an online platform, and the platform processes data from the user, then the user has the right to obtain contact details of the online platform. Moreover, the user has the right to know if the firm has collected data about the products the user viewed and is using this information to recommend other products to the user. This information puts the user in the position to contact the firm and enables the user to evaluate whether she agrees to the personal data processing.

The "Right to Access" entitles users to obtain copies of their personal data and further information about the personal data processing. In our example, the user who shops on the online platform can ask for a copy of the personal data that the online platform has stored about her, and for information about all personal data processing activities. Notably, this right forces firms that process users' personal data to document all of their processing activities. The Right to Access enables users to gain an in-depth understanding of which personal data the firm processes for what purpose, providing additional information that can assist them in evaluating whether to consent to having their personal data processed.

4.3.2 Rights Enabling Users to Change the Processing of Their Personal Data

The "Right to Rectification" provides a user with the opportunity to modify and correct potentially false or outdated personal data, which may harm the user otherwise. For example, in a situation in which a user's financial information was processed for the purpose of determining credit eligibility, it may be that the user was not solvent and, thus, not eligible for credit. However, once the user becomes solvent, the user may rectify the personal data about the insolvency, potentially preventing the information from harming future credit applications.

The "Right to Erasure" enables the user to force the firm that has processed the user's personal data to delete data that are not relevant for the purpose of the personal data processing. This right enables the user to negotiate with the firm about the relevance of personal data and puts the firm in the position to justify the personal data storage if the firm does not agree with the erasure. In our example, the user who became solvent may ask the firm to delete the past information about the user's insolvency because this personal data may not be relevant to assess the user's current solvency.

The "Right to Data Portability" enables the user to ask the firm to provide all personal data of the user to another firm in an accessible and machine-readable format. For example, a user may ask her current bank to transmit all her personal data to a new bank. This right decreases lock-in effects caused by so-called switching costs. Switching costs occur if the user faces costs caused by switching from one firm's service to another firm.

4.3.3 Rights Enabling Users to Restrict the Processing of Their Personal Data

The "Right to Restriction of Processing" enables a user to stop the processing of her personal data (temporarily) if the user doubts (i) the necessity to use the personal data to fulfill the purpose of the processing, (ii) the accuracy of (some of) the personal data used to achieve the purpose of the processing, or (iii) the lawfulness of the processing. Therefore, this right enables the user to take actual control of her own personal data and requires the firm to justify (i) the necessity, (ii) the accuracy and (iii) the lawfulness of the personal data processing. For example, suppose a user applies for credit, and an algorithm decides, on the basis of the user's personal data, whether the user should receive the credit. If the user determines that the personal data used to make this decision are unnecessary, incorrect, or illegally processed, then the user can demand that the website stops processing the personal data.

The "Right to Avoid Automated Decision-Making" ensures that the user has the right not to be subjected to a decision based solely upon automated processing, including profiling. This right applies primarily to cases in which decisions significantly impact the user, such as the refusal of an online credit application. More specifically, this right enables the user to demand that the data-processing firm assign humans to monitor decision-making processes that are otherwise carried out automatically, as humans may better detect mistakes in such processes. For example, if a user's credit application is rejected on the basis of an automated decision, then the user can object to the automated decision-making process and request that the firm (partially) re-evaluate this decision via a human.

The "Right to Object" entitles the user to object to the processing of personal data for marketing purposes, including marketing-related profiling. More specifically, this right enables users to ensure that they do not receive content or ads based on their past browsing behavior, demographics or interests. Therefore, this right enforces the user's fundamental right of informational self-determination. Returning to our example, suppose that the user who has applied for credit begins to receive advertisements based on the user's solvency rating. In this case, the user can object to this targeting strategy and can demand to see untargeted ads, which do not relate to the user's solvency rating. In order to override a user's objection to the processing of personal data, a firm must demonstrate compelling legitimate grounds for doing so.

4.4 Obligations for Firms that Process Personal Data

4.4.1 The Role of the Firm: Data Controller or Data Processor

According to the GDPR, a firm that handles a user's personal data is classified under one of two essential roles: "data controller" or "data processor". Each role entails specific responsibilities and obligations with regard to the processing of personal data—where a data controller has more obligations than a data processor. It is possible for a firm to be a data controller in some cases and a data processor in others, but never both simultaneously.

4.4.1.1 Definition of Data Controller

The GDPR defines in Article 4 point (7) that a firm is a data controller if the firm has the obligation of deciding why and how to process the personal data (the "purposes" and "means" of processing). Under the GDPR, the data controller faces several obligations, which we discuss in Section 4.4.2 and Section 4.4.3.

4.4.1.2 Definition of Data Processor

The GDPR outlines in Article 4 point (8) that a firm is a data processor if it processes personal data on behalf of a data controller. Thus, the data processor cannot decide why and how to process the personal data (the "purposes" and "means" of processing). We discuss the obligations of the data processor in Section 4.4.2.

4.4.1.3 Relationship Between Data Controller and Data Processor

By definition, a firm cannot be both a data controller and a data processor for the same personal data processing activity; it must be one or the other. Yet, a firm might be involved in multiple personal data processing activities (potentially even involving similar data)—and serve as a data processor in some activities and as a data controller in others.

For example, suppose that a demand-side platform (DSP) D receives a bid request from an ad exchange to bid on behalf of an advertiser A1 for a particular ad slot. That bid request comes with personal data such as the user ID (or cookie ID) for the user who will be exposed to the ad, the publisher P1 to which the ad slot belongs, and the information that the user is likely to be male. Concerning this bidding process, DSP D is a data processor because it processes personal data on behalf of the data controller (i.e., publisher P1, which sells the ad slot).

Assume further that DSP D also bids on behalf of another advertiser, advertiser A2, for an ad slot offered by a different publisher, P2. In this bidding process, advertiser A2 also receives personal data. DSP D remains a data processor for this bidding process because it processes personal data only on behalf of the data controller (i.e., publisher P2, which sells this ad slot).

However, DSP D turns into a data controller if it combines the personal information received from publishers P1 and P2. For example, DSP D could develop profiles about users that contain information that both publishers provided to sell these profiles to advertisers. The profiles are now the firm's "own" data. Therefore, the firm becomes a data controller.

4.4.2 Shared Obligations for Both the Data Controller and Data Processor

The GDPR stipulates several obligations with which both types of actors—the data controller and the data processor—must comply in order to engage in a particular activity involving the processing of personal data. Table 4 outlines the most important ones.

Table 4: *Overview of Obligations for both Data Controller and Data Processor under the GDPR*

Obligation	Data Controller	Data Processor
Processing Personal Data Based on a Legal Basis and Compliance with Associated Requirements	Yes	Yes
Documentation of Personal Data Processing	Yes	Yes
Implementation of Technical and Organizational Measures (Safeguarding Privacy by Design & Default)	Yes	Yes
Provision of Notification in Case of Data Breach	Yes	Yes

The first obligation—processing any personal data based on a legal basis—entails justifying the data processing activity by choosing an appropriate legal basis; the GDPR stipulates six arguments that constitute acceptable legal bases for personal data processing. The choice of a particular legal basis may be associated with additional requirements. Section 4.4.4 provides a detailed discussion of the various legal bases and the requirements associated with each one. While the data controller and data processor both need a legal basis, the choice of the legal basis is solely down to the controller. As such, the data processor relies on the legal basis chosen and established by the data controller.

The second obligation is for the actor to document all steps taken as part of the personal data processing activity, including the choice of a legal basis and the measures implemented to ensure compliance with all obligations. Third, the actor needs to implement appropriate technical and organizational measures to safeguard privacy by default and design. Finally, in the case of a data breach, the data controller is usually required to notify the personal data breach to the supervisory authority within 72 hours. In contrast, the data processor is required to notify the personal data breach to the data controller immediately.

For example, suppose that a firm has a database of customer email addresses (i.e., personal data), and it wants to send a newsletter to its customers to inform them about a sales event. To this end, the firm must "process" the email addresses, e.g., by gathering relevant email addresses from the database and sending the newsletter to these addresses. According to Table 4, the firm first needs a legal basis for this activity. Suppose that the firm chooses to rely on users' explicit consent as its legal basis (see Section 4.4.4.2.2 for a detailed discussion of explicit consent as a legal basis for data processing). In that case, the firm has to collect users' explicit consent to have their email addresses used for receiving newsletters. Moreover, once the firm has chosen explicit consent as its legal basis, it needs to fulfill all associated requirements stipulated in the GDPR—e.g., informing the user of the purpose of personal data processing prior to requesting consent.

Second, the firm needs to document all its activities with regard to the processing of users' email addresses. Notably, in line with the user's "Right to Access" (Section 4.3.1), if the user requests this documentation, the firm must provide it. Third, the firm must implement appropriate technical and organizational measures to safeguard personal data. For example, the firm could encrypt the files in the database to protect the email addresses from being stolen, or store more sensitive personal data about the users in a different database with pseudonymized email addresses. Fourth, the firm needs to inform the supervising authority in the case of a data breach.

If the firm hires a digital marketing agency to promote its sales event, then the marketing agency acts as a data processor. As such, it relies on the legal basis, i.e., explicit consent, chosen and established by the firm. However, similarly to the firm, the marketing agency needs to document all personal data processing activities, implement appropriate technical and organizational measures to safeguard personal data, and inform the data controller in case of a data breach.

4.4.3 Obligations for Data Controller but not Data Processor

The GDPR stipulates several obligations that apply to the data controller but not to the data processor. Table 5 outlines the most important ones.

Table 5: *Overview of Obligations only for Data Controller and not for Data Processor*

Obligation	Data Controller	Data Processor
Selection of Purposes of Personal Data Processing	Yes	No
Justification of Relevance of Personal Data	Yes	No
Assurance of Data Processor's GDPR Compliance	Yes	No

These additional obligations include a requirement for the data controller to select the purposes of processing personal data before processing the personal data. Continuing our previous example, for the firm processing consumers' email addresses, the purpose of data processing might be "informing customers about a sales event". An additional obligation that the data controller must fulfill is to justify the relevance of all personal data that the data controller processes. In our example, the firm needs to be able to justify the relevance of processing the email addresses and any other personal data involved in this processing activity, such as names. If the firm is unable to justify the relevance, then the user might rely on the "Right to Erasure" to have the irrelevant personal data deleted. Regarding the firm's purpose to inform customers about a sales event, the firm might justify the processing of email addresses by referring to the requirement that the firm needs the customers' email addresses to send them emails about the sales event. A further obligation for the data controller is to ensure the compliance of the data processor with the GDPR. So, if the firm relies on a marketing agency to inform its customers about the sales event, the data controller needs to make sure, that the data processor fulfills all obligations of the GDPR regarding the specific personal data processing activities.

4.4.4 Obligations with Respect to Legal Bases

As noted in Section 4.4.2, both the data controller and data processor are required to base the processing of personal data on a legal basis. Article 6 of the GDPR, "Lawfulness of processing", defines six possible legal bases for data processing, and a firm must be able to document the presence of one of these legal bases in order to be able to lawfully process personal data for a specific purpose. The applicability of each legal basis varies across industries. In what follows, we elaborate on each legal basis based on the legal definitions made within the GDPR, classifying them according to whether or not they are relevant for the advertising industry.

4.4.4.1 Legal Bases not Relevant for Advertising

4.4.4.1.1 Vital Interest

The legal basis of vital interest applies to processing activities that are necessary to "protect vital interests of the user or another natural person" (Art. 6 point (1d), GDPR). A vital interest exists if personal data processing aids in protecting a person's life (Recital 46, GDPR). In other words, this legal basis applies to processing activities necessary for matters of life and death, such as medical emergencies: If an individual has life-threatening injuries from an accident and medics admit her to a hospital, then the processing of the individual's personal data, e.g., to admit the patient to the hospital, is necessary to protect the individual's life.

Due to its nature, the legal basis of vital interest does not apply to firms within the online advertisement industry. Indeed, online banner advertisements cannot convincingly be a matter of life and death.

4.4.4.1.2 Public Interest

Public interest serves as a legal basis for processing activities that are necessary to enable tasks that are of "public interest or in the exercise of official authority" (Art. 6 point (1e), GDPR). For example, a public interest may exist if the firm is a public authority. Another example might be the processing of personal data, e.g., the name and address of an individual, for national elections, as the processing serves the public.

Similarly to vital interest, public interest is unlikely to apply as an appropriate legal basis for firms within the online advertising industry. Unless firms are official authorities, online banner advertisements are unlikely to serve a public interest.

4.4.4.1.3 Legal Obligation

The legal basis of legal obligation applies if personal data processing is "necessary for compliance with a legal obligation" that binds a data controller or processor (Art. 6 point (1c), GDPR). An example of a processing activity based on a legal obligation is if a court processes personal data when inviting witnesses.

Due to its nature, the legal basis of legal obligation is unlikely to serve as the most appropriate legal basis for personal data processing within the online advertising industry.

4.4.4.1.4 Contract Fulfillment

The legal basis of contract fulfillment applies if a data controller or processor has to process personal data in order to enable a user to enter into or complete a contract (Art. 6 point (1b), GDPR). Such a legal basis might be applicable, for example, to a retailer selling clothes online: To complete a transaction—i.e., enter into a contract with the retailer—the user needs to provide personal data such as a name, shipping address, and credit card information. Without the processing of such information, the contract between the two parties (provision of clothing in exchange for payment) cannot be fulfilled.

Data controllers may claim the legal basis of contract fulfillment when setting so-called "strictly necessary" cookies on their websites. Strictly necessary cookies, also called technically necessary cookies, are essential for a website to function and for the user to use the website's features. Such cookies include, for example, those that enable websites to process payment information or to save items placed in a shopping cart.

Although contract fulfillment can be an applicable legal basis for using (strictly necessary) cookies, it currently does not serve as a legal basis for personal data processing for the purpose of online advertising. More specifically, cookies used for online advertising cannot be categorized as strictly necessary. Thus, contract fulfillment currently cannot serve as a legal basis for firms in the advertising industry. With the rise of the PUR model (see Section 5.2.2.2), however, contract fulfillment might play a more important role.

4.4.4.2 Legal Bases Relevant for Advertising

4.4.4.2.1 Legitimate Interest

Firms can apply the legal basis of legitimate interest if the personal data processing is "necessary for the legitimate interest pursued by a data controller or a third party, except where such interests are overridden by the interests or fundamental rights and freedoms of the [user]" (Art. 6 point (1f), GDPR). To be able to claim this legal basis, a data controller must provide documentation on a case-by-case basis showing that its own legitimate interests in processing a user's data outweigh the user's interests in not having the data processed.

If a firm uses the legitimate interest claim as a legal basis for carrying out personal data processing activities, the firm needs to be transparent about the personal data processing activities and further inform the user that and how they can object to these activities (Art. 21, GDPR). Therefore, loosely speaking, legitimate interest represents the opt-out approach of personal data processing: If the user does not opt-out of personal data processing based on legitimate interest, data controllers can process personal data.

A firm may make the argument that data processing for marketing activities serves a legitimate interest. For a publisher, for example, collecting and using personal data can enable behaviorally targeted ads to be served to users, thereby generating revenues for the publisher (which, in turn, may offer its content for free to users—suggesting that the user's interests are not harmed). At the same time, if a user might not reasonably expect personal data processing, it is harder for a firm to argue that a legitimate interest to process the personal data exists.

Thus, legitimate interest may be a legal basis that firms can use to justify the processing of users' personal data. However, the Data Protection Authority responsible for a firm has to decide upon its applicability on a case-by-case basis. Yet, the applicability for the legal basis of legitimate interest for tracking activities will likely be limited in certain countries. For example, Germany eliminated the possibility to use legitimate interest for online tracking technologies with the Telecommunications and Telemedia Data Protection Act (TTDSG) that entered into force in December 2021.

4.4.4.2.2 Consent

The GDPR regulates the legal basis of consent in Article 6 point (1a) and in Article 7. A user may give consent for "one or more specific purposes" of personal data processing activities. Valid consent under the GDPR stipulates a privacy-preserving default, the opt-in approach, that we call "explicit consent". This opt-in approach stipulates that without action by the user, the user does not give consent. Additionally, consent needs to be:

- **Freely given:** The user should not be or feel persuaded to give her consent. The consent must be given voluntarily, i.e., offering a real choice to the user. Above all, access to content or a data controller's offering must not be conditional on consent. Yet, there have been some cases in which DPAs allow the access to content being conditional on consent. Such a case would be the presence of an equivalent paid alternative (as, e.g., the Austrian DPA ruled in 2019, Datenschutzbehörde 2019).

- **Specific:** The user has to give consent for specific purposes and third parties.

- **Informed:** Before giving consent, a user needs to have access to information about the personal data processing and to be able to understand what the user is consenting to. This information should include the nature of personal data processed, the purposes of the personal data processing, who will have access to the data, and how the data controller safeguards the data.

- **Unambiguous:** There must be no doubt whether a user has consented and to what a user has consented.

- **Made with a clear affirmative action:** The user has to actively and explicitly give her consent. Without action by a user, the data controller cannot obtain consent.

Furthermore, after a user has given consent for a specific personal data processing activity, the user has the right to revoke the consent. It must be as easy for the user to revoke her consent as it is to provide consent. The user must be able to withdraw previously

given consent at any point in time. If a firm fulfills all of these requirements, it has obtained the user's valid consent.

An example of valid consent under the GDPR would be this scenario: A data controller
informs the user about the personal data processing, the purposes of that personal data
processing, and the third parties that will have access to the data. After viewing this
explanation, the user can tick several un-ticked boxes for each purpose of the personal
data processing separately. The data controller informs the user that and how she can
withdraw consent at any time. A user can access the service even if she denies consent.

To summarize, consent is a legal basis that firms within the online advertising industry
can use for personal data processing. Under the GDPR, consent is contingent on an opt-in
approach. This approach likely makes personal data processing transparent to the user.

4.5 Specific Conditions Regarding Legal Bases for User Tracking Technologies

As the GDPR affects all processing activities that enable individuals to be identified, the
tracking technologies discussed in previous sections—including login data, digital fingerprinting, and cookies—are all within the scope of the GDPR. As such, these technologies
should presumably be subject to the conditions outlined above regarding the applicability of the various legal bases. Yet, recent state court decisions have imposed additional
restrictions with regard to the use of tracking technologies in the advertising industry
specifically. In particular, the applicability of legitimate interest as a legal basis—one of
the two legal bases that are relevant for the advertising industry (the other is consent;
see Section 4.4.4.2)—has been limited with regard to tracking technologies that serve
advertising purposes. For example, in May 2020, the German Federal Court of Justice
reinforced the Planet49 ruling by the European Court of Justice of October 2019, which
effectively limits the use of legitimate interest as a legal basis for tracking technologies,
instead requiring that data controllers and processors obtain valid consent (Information
Commissioner's Office 2019).

The EU tried to mitigate uncertainties about the applicability of legal bases and the
practical implementation of the GDPR's requirements for the digital world by drafting
another regulation, the ePrivacy Regulation, which we discuss in Section 9.3.3. This regulation intends to extend but not replace the GDPR's requirements in online settings.
In particular, it should regulate questions and uncertainties regarding online marketing. However, this regulation has no finalized draft as of June 2021. Consequently, it is
currently difficult to claim legitimate interest as a legal basis for user tracking in online

advertising. This situation might change once the ePrivacy Regulation is finalized—though this is not very likely.

4.6 Legal Bases for Tracking under other Privacy Laws

Though this chapter focuses on the EU's GDPR, it is important to acknowledge the numerous other privacy laws worldwide that handle various aspects of privacy—in some cases, similarly to the GDPR, and in others, slightly differently. In Table 6, we compare some of these laws—specifically, with regard to their handling of legal bases for the processing of personal data in general, and for the use of tracking technologies in the online advertising industry specifically.

Table 6 shows that most major privacy laws worldwide require the same legal bases for tracking that the GDPR requires. Some privacy laws even allow for legal bases other than those allowed by the GDPR (Brazil's LGPD, India's PDPB, China's PIPL). Moreover, most privacy laws (LGPD, PDPB, PIPL, and Thailand's PDPA, in addition to the GDPR) entail similar criteria for valid consent—namely, users must provide consent explicitly (an opt-in approach), in a free, specific, informed, and unambiguous manner (see Section 4.4.4.2.2). Thus, any firm worldwide that caters to users based in the EU, Brazil, India, China, or Thailand must comply with these requirements for consent. California's Consumer Privacy Act (CCPA) is the only major privacy law that stipulates an opt-out approach to consent, i.e., users' consent is assumed unless they actively object to personal data processing activities.

The various countries also differ in terms of the penalties they impose for infringement of privacy laws. A firm that infringes on the GDPR can be required to pay a fine of up to 4% of its global annual turnover or €20 million, whichever amount is higher. Under the LGPD, fines can reach up to 2% of a firm's global annual turnover. The PDPA and CCPA, in turn, specify flat sums at which firms can be fined: up to 5 million Thai Baht ($150,000) for the PDPA and up to $7,500 for the CCPA. For grave violation against the PIPL, a firm must pay a fine of up to 5% of its annual turnover or 50 million Yuan (around $8 million). Moreover, the directly responsible person in charge can be fined under PIPL between 10 thousand and 1 million Yuan ($1,600 to $160,000). So, China's privacy law (PIPL) is roughly as strict as the GDPR in terms of fines, the legal bases and the requirement of consent from the user to use their personal data.

Table 6: *Comparison of Legal Bases for Tracking in Major Privacy Laws Worldwide*

Privacy Law	Possible Legal Bases	Possible Legal Bases for Tracking
GDPR (EU)	• Consent • Legitimate Interest • Legal Obligation • Contract Fulfillment • Public Interest • Vital Interest	• Consent (opt-in approach) • Legitimate Interest
CCPA (California)	• Consent	• Consent (opt-out approach)
LGPD (Brazil)	• Consent • Legitimate Interest • Legal Obligation • Regular Exercise of Rights • Contract Fulfillment • Credit Protection • Public Interest • Vital Interest • Health Protection • Research Activities	• Consent (opt-in approach) • Legitimate Interest
PDPB (India)	• Consent • State Performance • Legal Obligation to State • Legal Obligation to Court • Vital Interest (Medical Services only) • Health Service (in Epidemics) • Individual Safety (for Disasters) • Employment Purposes • Legitimate Interest (limited to specific situations)	• Consent (opt-in approach)
PDPA (Thailand)	• Consent • Legitimate Interest • Legal Obligation • Contract Fulfillment • Public Interest • Vital Interest	• Consent (opt-in approach) • Legitimate Interest
PIPL (China)	• Consent • Legal Obligation • Contract Fulfillment • Public Interest • Vital Interest • Disclosed Information (disclosed by data subjects themselves or otherwise lawfully disclosed)	• Consent (opt-in approach) • Consent (opt-in separately for sensitive information)

4.7 Main Takeaways

The main takeaways from Section 4 are:

- The GDPR is a privacy law of the European Union applicable to all European firms and all firms processing personal data of European citizens.

- The GDPR aims to give users more control over their personal data by defining user rights to understand, change, and restrict the personal data processing.

- The GDPR increases responsibilities for all actors who process personal data. For a given data-processing activity, the GDPR defines an actor as either a data processor or a data controller, where data controllers have more obligations than data processors do. Data controllers are also responsible for the legal compliance of the cooperating data processors.

- The GDPR stipulates that in order to process personal data, a firm must specify a legal basis for personal data processing. For firms in the advertising industry, the two applicable legal bases are legitimate interest and consent.

- Loosely speaking, legitimate interest represents the opt-out approach for getting permission for personal data processing, whereas consent represents an opt-in approach.

- Even though the GDPR identifies both consent and legitimate interest as applicable legal bases for firms in the advertising industry, courts have reduced the applicability of legitimate interest, consequently favoring consent.

5

Effects of the Requirement for a Legal Basis for Data Processing

Among the numerous changes introduced by the GDPR with regard to the processing of personal data—including new rights for users, as well as new obligations for firms—the most meaningful change for the advertising industry is perhaps the requirement for firms to supply a legal basis for data processing. As discussed above, in the advertising industry, this requirement implies that firms must inform the user about all processing activities, including tracking, and obtain the user's permission for these activities—either explicit, in cases in which consent serves as the legal basis; or implicit, in the form of non-objection to data processing, in cases in which legitimate interest serves as the legal basis.

Before the introduction of the GDPR, the default was that actors in the online advertising industry could process the user's personal data at will—and users who wished to reduce or prevent tracking could only do so by installing anti-tracking software or altering their browsers' settings. Accordingly, the requirement to obtain user permission for data processing constitutes a profound change in the operations of the online advertising industry. This section elaborates on how this change affects the various firms operating in the advertising market, the users themselves, and the interplay between them. We distinguish between effects that are independent of the user's decision, i.e., granting or denying permission for data processing (Section 5.1), and those dependent on the user's decision (Section 5.2).

5.1 Effects Independent of the Outcome of the User's Decision

5.1.1 Effects of Asking for Permission

5.1.1.1 Effects on Firms Operating in the Online Advertising Industry

In practice, a common approach by which publishers inform users of data processing activities and obtain their permission for such activities is by implementing "cookie banners" (named after the predominant tracking technology, see Section 3.1), also referred to as "consent banners". A publisher displays a cookie banner to the user when she first visits its website. Figure 10 shows an example of such a cookie banner.

Figure 10: *Example of a Cookie Banner (here: www.ecodibergamo.it)*

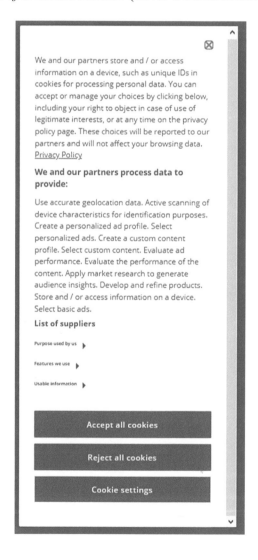

The crucial challenge for the publisher is to implement a cookie banner that is compliant with the GDPR, i.e., provides comprehensive information, and that is user-friendly, i.e., does not deter the user. Furthermore, this information needs to cover the purposes of personal data processing and identify all firms that get access to the data. Thus, the cookie banner can become tedious to read for the user, which can conflict with the user's aim, namely, to consume the website's content instantly.

In order to develop and implement a user-friendly and GDPR-compliant cookie banner from scratch, a publisher would need to invest in human resources like lawyers, data privacy experts, user experience designers, and web developers. Yet, a new actor has emerged to assist publishers, particularly smaller ones, in producing such banners in a less costly manner: namely, firms that offer Consent Management Platforms (CMPs). We describe them in more detail in Section 6.1.

5.1.1.2 Effects on the User

When a user visits a publisher's website for the first time, the user's browser has to load the cookie banner and the website's content. Loading a cookie banner takes several seconds (Hils et al. 2020) and increases the time until the user can access the publisher's content. Thus, the presence of a cookie banner can impair users' online experience, particularly when users do not have a fast Internet connection.

Furthermore, the user needs to respond to the cookie banner that requests permission for personal data processing. Since there is no single universal design for cookie banners, the user faces various cookie banners across websites (Degeling et al. 2019). These cookie banners differ in several dimensions, such as the position on the website, the number of layers (nested sites of the banner), and the buttons to select. Given the interest of the online advertising industry in getting permission for all purposes, particularly tracking, profiling and targeting (Section 3.2), the publisher has an incentive to lead the user to an "accept all" decision. Therefore, cookie banners are often designed so as to make it easy for the user to click an "accept all" or "allow all" button, i.e., to grant permission for all specified purposes of the publisher. Such a design might entail, for example, presenting an "accept all" option on the first layer of the cookie banner, i.e., the part of the cookie banner that the user instantly sees.

Compared with granting permission, denying permission for data processing is often less straightforward for the user. For example, many cookie banners do not provide a "deny all" button (Sanchez-Rola et al. 2019) on the first layer and instead require the user to open a second layer, e.g., by clicking on a "settings" button (Schmitt 2021).

Suppose the user wants to make a more differentiated decision and only wants to give or deny permission for specific purposes, such as the use of personal data for ad performance measurement. In that case, the user also needs to access the second layer and go through all the specified purposes, selecting the ones that are acceptable to her. Thus, the user needs to process more information and click more times than she would have to had she selected the "accept all" option (or the "deny all" option, if available). This scenario illustrates that a decision deviating from the "accept all" option increases the user's effort and the amount of time she must wait until she can access the website's content—thereby impairing the user's online experience.

In Section 8.4, we present an empirical study that provides evidence for the number of decisions a user typically makes when faced with a cookie banner, and the average time spent making each decision. Notably, developers have created various non-commercial tools to streamline the decision-making process, with the aim of preventing cookie banners from impairing the user experience. We discuss these tools in Section 6.2.

Summing up, users gain benefits from the requirement for publishers to ensure that they have permission (i.e. a legal basis) for data processing, as this requirement increases users' control over their personal data—enabling users to deny permission, or provide it only for specific purposes. Yet, at the same time, this requirement entails costs for the user, who may be subjected to a lengthy and potentially annoying decision process. For some users, the benefits of control over one's data may outweigh the costs—whereas for others, the opposite may be the case.

5.1.2 Effects of Documenting and Managing Permissions

5.1.2.1 Effects on Firms Operating in the Online Advertising Industry

Regardless of whether the user has granted or denied permission for personal data processing, the publisher must document the request for permission and the user's decision. This obligation comes with considerable costs to the publisher, requiring, for example, investments in technological infrastructure, processes, and personnel.

To illustrate these documentation costs, consider a publisher such as the German news site Focus Online (www.focus.de). According to assessments by AGOF (a German association of online marketers), Focus Online has approximately 25 million unique monthly users (as of September 2021, www.agof.de/?wpfb_dl=8454). Suppose that, in a given month, the publisher lacks information regarding permission decisions for about 25% of users—for example, because these users are new, or deleted their cookies. Focus Online then has to request permission from these users and store the information regarding their decisions. This process yields 6.25 million decisions per month (=25% · 25 million users per month · 1 decision per user). Let us further assume that Focus Online collaborates with and therefore transfers personal data to 100 other actors (such as a retargeting agency or an ad exchange)—for which it must also request and store each user's permission decision (see Section 7 for more information on how these steps are accomplished). Thus, Focus Online needs to request and store 625 million decisions per month (=6.25 million decisions per month and actor · 100 actors) for these actors. Overall, Focus Online needs to document 6.25 million decisions (for itself) and 625 million decisions (for other actors), in total 631.25 million decisions. The online advertising industry, particularly IAB Europe, created the Transparency and Consent Framework (TCF) to support this documentation process. We describe the TCF in Section 7.

In addition to the documentation costs, the GDPR induces other costs from processes that we refer to as the management of permissions for data processing. For example, the GDPR endows the user with the rights to understand, change, and restrict personal data processing (Section 4.3). Thus, the publisher needs to enable the user to retract or alter the permission for processing personal data and be able to delete the collected data of a user at any point in time. Subsequently, we outline the resulting costs using the example of a publisher. However, these costs occur similarly to all vendors that process the user's data on behalf of the publisher.

Returning to our example, let us assume that, in a given month, only 0.5% of all Focus Online's users retract their permission and request the deletion of their personal data. In this case, Focus Online would need to provide data for 125,000 users (= 0.5% · 25 million users). Suppose this provision is a manual process, i.e., a service or back-office employee individually updates the database for each user's data and then sends each user an individual email. Then, the resulting personnel cost would be extremely high. For example, assuming a minimum duration of 3 minutes per user, the resulting total duration of this work would be 375,000 minutes (=125,000 users · 3 minutes per user), i.e., 6,250 hours, equivalent to 260 days or 8.5 months of non-stop work just to respond to all requests from one month. In a country like Germany, where the gross minimum wage per hour in 2021 is 9.50€, the corresponding gross cost for personnel is equal to 59,375€ per month, or 712,500€ per year. These estimates represent a lower bound, given that the calculation was based on the minimum wage and neglected non-wage labor costs such as health insurance. Therefore, it seems beneficial for firms to invest in processes and IT infrastructure that automate the described process.

The fashion retailer Zalando is an example of a firm that enables users to submit an online request for information about and deletion of their stored data, as Figure 11 illustrates. Notably, even this technologically advanced retailer outlines that it can take up to 30 days (the maximum allowed duration) to provide a user with the stored data. Thus, it is evident that a publisher might incur immense costs to comply with the user's right to information. Overall, we can conclude that the GDPR has induced new and substantial costs for the online advertising industry.

Figure 11: *Example of a Data Request (here: Member Area of Zalando.de)*

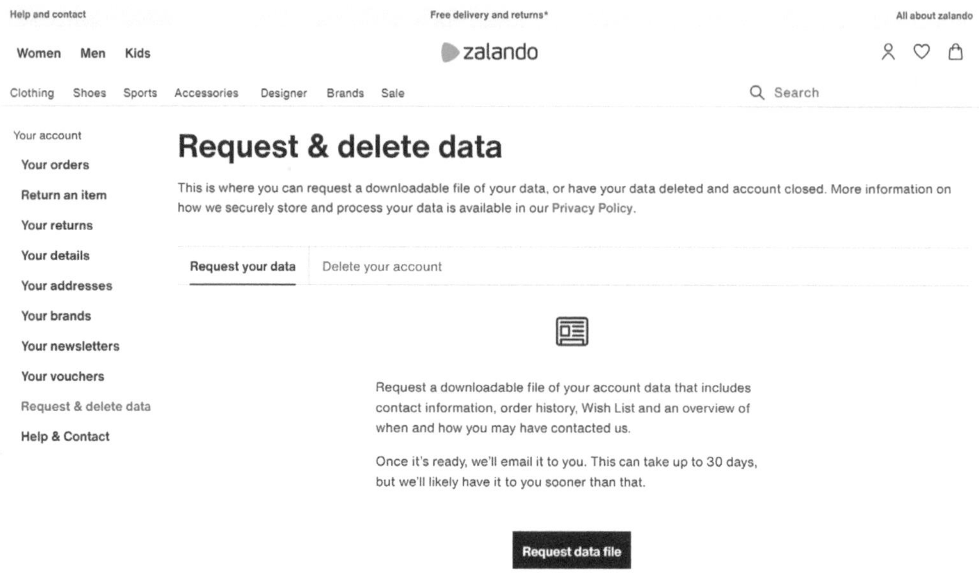

5.1.2.2 Effects on the User

Documenting all firms that collect the user's personal data is crucial for enabling the user to exercise full control over these data. Assume, for example, that a user decides to apply online for new health insurance. Some online insurance providers might have already tracked the user online and targeted the users with ads. The user may, at one time, have granted permission to the various health-related publishers to process her data, e.g., for the purpose of receiving personalized content. The insurance providers can use the data that was previously collected for advertising to tailor their offers (O'Neil 2016), e.g., set the price of the offer. Such data might include, for example, the health-related publishers the user visited, which exact content the user viewed, and on which health-related ads the user clicked. But now, before the health insurance application, the user wishes to retract the permission and have the collected data deleted. Therefore, the user needs to know precisely which health-related publishers collected her data and which other actors were involved in the data processing, i.e., which other actors also got access to the data.

Assume that 10% of all unique publishers the user visits are health-related. If we further assume that the average user visits 50 unique publishers per month, then the user is estimated to visit 5 unique health-related publishers per month (= 10% of health-related publishers · 50 unique publishers). If each of these publishers has connections to 100 other actors, the user would need to keep a monthly record of 5 publishers and 250 other actors (=5 publishers · 100 other actors per publisher of which 50% overlap). Thus, we conclude that the user also faces high costs for managing her permissions.

5.2 Effects Dependent on the Outcome of the User's Decision

We continue by outlining how users' decisions to grant versus deny permission for data processing affect firms operating in the advertising industry, as well as the users themselves. We focus on two extreme cases: the case in which the user grants permission for all personal data processing (e.g., chooses the "accept all" option in response to a cookie banner); and the case in which the user denies permission for all personal data processing (e.g., chooses the "deny all" option).

5.2.1 Effects of Granting Permission

5.2.1.1 Effects on Firms Operating in the Online Advertising Industry

If a user grants the publisher permission for all processing of personal data (e.g., by choosing the "accept all" option), then the publisher (and other actors with which it collaborates) can track, profile, and target the user for the purposes the publisher has specified. This level of access is similar to what the publisher would have been able to achieve before the GDPR—with the difference being that the publisher has the user's informed permission to engage in its data processing activities, and has made these activities more transparent to the user. Indeed, in this case, the publisher has a legal basis that supports the lawfulness of its personal data processing activities, in accordance with the GDPR's specifications.

Given the many advantages that the online advertising industry derives from tracking, profiling, and targeting, an advertiser will likely prefer to display ads with a publisher where users can be tracked, profiled, and targeted rather than with a publisher for which these practices are not possible. Thus, the publisher gains a competitive advantage from having a large share of users who provide consent to tracking, profiling and targeting. The percentage of users who permit such activities is referred to as the publisher's "consent rate" (in %).

5.2.1.2 Effects on the User

A user who chooses the "accept all" option receives targeted ads and personalized content. Such personalization enhances the likelihood that the user will be exposed to ads and content that are "relevant", i.e., aligned with her interests (Boerman et al. 2017). Increased relevance of ads and content, in turn, improves the user's online experience.

Personalization of ads and content comes at a certain cost to users. First, when more firms have access to a user's personal data, the risk of potential misuse of the data increases. Moreover, if the user wishes to actively keep track of the firms that process his data—e.g., so that he will be able to delete the data later on—then any provision of consent translates into additional effort that the user must invest. Recall, however, that the user grants or denies consent on a case-by-case basis to each publisher—and thus can mitigate these concerns, to some extent, by selecting the individual publishers to whom he wishes to grant the opportunity to feature targeted ads and personalized content. For example, such consent may benefit the user when she visits publishers that provide content directly related to her hobbies (e.g., travel magazines) but may be less useful on other types of websites.

5.2.2 Effects of Denying Permission

5.2.2.1 Effects on Firms Operating in the Online Advertising Industry

If a user chooses to deny consent for any data processing, the publisher (and other actors with whom the publisher collaborates) cannot track, profile, or target the individual user. The inability to track users limits advertisers' activity (in comparison to the situation pre-GDPR, or, alternatively, situations in which users provide consent). For example, the advertiser cannot "retarget" the user—a term that refers to displaying ads to users who have previously visited an advertiser's website without purchasing. Moreover, the advertiser has no information about which ads a user saw in the past. Thus, the advertiser is not able to conduct recency or frequency capping and cannot learn about the user's interactions with specific ads at different points in time, for example, for attribution modeling. Consequently, advertising along the specific customer journey of a user is almost impossible. At best, the advertiser can target groups of users, such as in contextual targeting or when advertising at different points in time.

The inability to target users is likely to diminish the performance of the advertiser's ads and to increase ad wastage. These effects, in turn, may (i) diminish the advertiser's willingness to pay for online advertising; and (ii) provide the advertiser with an incentive to shift its budget to other types of advertising. These reactions ultimately decrease ad prices. Empirical evidence suggests that ad prices are 40%-50% lower for users for whom tracking is disabled, as compared with users for whom tracking is enabled (Johnson, Shriver, and Du 2020; Laub, Miller, and Skiera 2022).

Lower ad prices imply less revenue for the publisher—meaning that the publisher has fewer means to finance the website's content. Consequently, the publisher's content quality decreases, potentially attracting fewer users (Shiller, Waldfogel, and Ryan 2018). This decrease in the number of users, in turn, reduces the number of ad impressions that the publisher can sell—further diminishing the publisher's ad revenue. However, viewing fewer ads, for example, by blocking some ads using an ad blocker but allowlisting others, can lead to a higher news consumption (Yan, Miller, and Skiera 2022).

There are notable examples of publishers that increased their revenue without us-er-tracking, such as Netherland's public broadcaster (Nederlandse Publieke Omroep (NPO)). In essence, NPO draw benefits from two developments when refraining from third-party tracking technologies. First, they improved their contextual targeting capabilities, which attracted advertisers to buy NPO's ad inventory even without user-tracking. Second, they cut out ad tech vendors that were involved in user-tracking and behaviorally targeted ads. Thus, NPO managed to increase their revenue without requiring the consent of the users. However, the well-documented empirical results of Johnson, Shriver, and Du (2020) and Laub, Miller, and Skiera (2022) point in a different direction.

A lack of permission to track users may further diminish the attractiveness of the publisher's content—and thereby decrease its user base—because of the publisher's inability to (i) personalize the content of the website (e.g., by personalizing the content ranking) and (ii) measure the success of the website's content for an individual user (e.g., Ho and Bodoff 2014). For example, without permission for tracking, the publisher can no longer observe when and where a user leaves the website and make improvements to retain the user's interest.

Together, these effects indicate that a user's denial of permission for personal data processing —resulting from the GDPR's requirement for a legal basis for data processing—induces a threat of revenue loss for actors in the advertising industry. In particular, the advertiser experiences more ad wastage—though it may be able to offset such wastage by paying lower ad prices. The publisher, in turn, suffers a loss, with the precise effect largely depending on the consent rate of the publisher. In other words, the publisher is more affected by the GDPR than the advertiser, and the publisher is the actor with a greater interest in obtaining the user's permission for tracking.

5.2.2.2 Effects on the User

For the user, an obvious consequence of denying consent for personal data processing is exposure to non-personalized content and ads—which may be less relevant to the user's interests compared with personalized content and ads (which the user would be more likely to have viewed before the GDPR, when tracking was the default). A consequence that is less obvious for most users is the possibility of a decrease in the quality of free online content—as a result of lower ad revenues, according to the logic outlined above.

Publishers might further respond to decreasing ad revenues by charging for their content, or by adopting innovative approaches such as so-called cookie paywalls (referred to by some German and Austrian publishers as the "PUR model")—which offers users a choice between either accepting the website's tracking or paying for a tracking-free (and sometimes even ad-free) version of the website (Müller-Tribbensee, Miller, and Skiera 2022). The PUR model has gained popularity, especially among content providers such as the news website *Washington Post* (see Figure 12). Yet, it is not entirely clear whether this model is compatible with the GDPR's requirement that, to serve as a legal basis for tracking, the user's consent must be freely given (meaning that the user's capacity to access a website cannot be contingent on the provision of consent). Indeed, requiring the user to accept tracking in order to access free content seems to negate the idea of freely given consent. Yet publishers might argue that the user is, in fact, free to make a choice—as she can access the content while still avoiding tracking by paying the publisher's stated price. Some Data Protection Authorities, such as the ones in Austria and in Hamburg, have decided that the PUR model is valid as long as the price for the content is reasonably low. In this case, the user is considered to have a choice between paying with data or with money for the publisher's content.

Figure 12: *Example of the PUR Model (here: www.washingtonpost.com)*

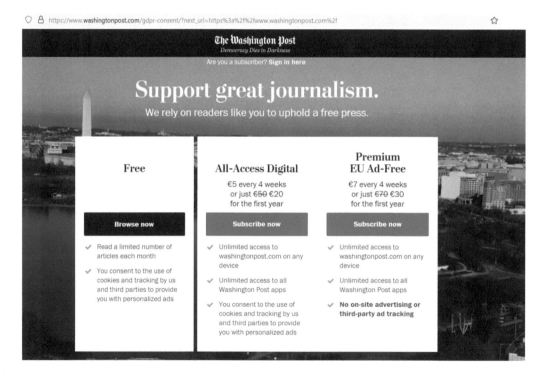

Several industry actors have proposed an alternative model in which, instead of paying to access a publisher's website with data or money, users sell the rights to process their personal data, i.e., allow tracking, in exchange for money. For some users, this approach could be an attractive alternative to denying permission. A significant obstacle to this approach is that the user typically does not know the data's value (Lischka and Kenning 2020). Moreover, the opportunity to sell data in exchange for money is not universally available; firms adopting this model have begun to emerge only recently. We discuss industry initiatives that picked up this approach and tackled these obstacles in Section 9.1.

5.3 Main Takeaways

The main takeaways from Section 5 are:

- The requirement for a legal basis for data processing in the advertising industry—in the form of either explicit permission (consent) for data processing or implicit permission (legitimate interest)—provides users with more control over their personal data, enabling them to determine how much tracking, profiling, and targeting to allow, if any. Yet this benefit comes with costs for actors in the advertising industry, as well as for the users themselves.

- Regardless of whether users provide or deny permission for data processing, publishers face high costs for requesting such permission (e.g., through cookie banners) and managing information on users' decisions.

- The very need to decide whether to provide permission, as well as to track and manage such decisions, also entails costs for users, which may worsen the user's online experience.

- If the user grants (as opposed to denying) permission for data processing, the user likely receives ads and content of higher relevance, but shares more personal data with a variety of firms, which represents a loss of privacy.

- If the user denies permission,

  - the advertiser has less data to improve online advertising performance and becomes less willing to pay for online advertising;

  - the publisher, in turn, faces a threat of lower revenue from online advertising to finance its free content. Thus, a high consent rate represents a competitive advantage for a publisher;

  - the quantity and quality of the content that the user can access for free may be lower than they would have been had the user provided permission.

6

Consent Management Tools

In the previous section, we discussed how the GDPR's requirement for a legal basis for data processing—which, for actors in the advertising industry, implies a need to get the user's explicit or implicit permission for data processing—entails costs to both publishers and users. In what follows, we elaborate on tools that have been developed to mitigate these costs. For the publishers, there are Consent Management Platforms (CMPs), which is software often combined with services, and for users there is software, often in the form of a browser extension.

6.1 Consent Management Platforms (CMPs) for the Online Advertising Industry

A CMP is software that provides publishers with technical support in obtaining and managing users' permissions with regard to data processing. It also centralizes information about users' permissions, such as when, where (on which website) and what permission occurred. Table 7 illustrates the core functionalities of a CMP (Gradow and Greiner 2021). Though some publishers implement and run their own CMPs in-house, others rely on external firms, called CMP-providers, that implement and run CMPs for them.

Table 7: *Core Functionalities of a Consent Management Platform (CMP)*

Aspect of User Permission for Data Processing	Core Functionalities of CMP
Asking for Permission	• Inform the user about the processing of personal data via a cookie banner.
	• Request user's permission to process personal data via the cookie banner.
	• Store the user's permission decisions.
Managing Permission	• Share the user's permission decisions with other actors.
	• Provide user interface to change permission.
	• Document all permission decisions for audit purposes.

6.1.1 Use of Consent Management Platform (CMP) for Requesting User Permission for Data Processing

A CMP provides publishers with the technology to create and display a request for permission, in the form of a cookie banner that is displayed to the user.

Some CMP-providers offer various additional services for enhancing the request for consent. First, some CMP-providers offer A/B testing to optimize the design of the cookie banner, so as to increase the likelihood of obtaining the user's consent. Such optimization includes testing variations in design elements such as the position of the banner or the color scheme, as well as variations in the text used to lead the user towards accepting tracking. On the basis of its experience with various publishers, the CMP-provider gains crucial knowledge about optimal cookie banner design—knowledge that enhances the value of its services and makes it an essential actor in the online advertising industry.

A second service that CMP-providers offer is the detection of hidden trackers. Under the GDPR, the publisher must inform the user about, and obtain permission for, all tracking activities on its website. Yet, the publisher might not be aware of all implemented trackers. Specifically, some trackers, called "piggyback trackers", hide within other trackers. For example, a third-party cookie on publisher A's website might have a connection to another third-party cookie that publisher A is unaware of. If publisher

A fails to get permission for the activities of this hidden tracker, it will be in violation of the GDPR and risk incurring high fines. CMP-providers that detect hidden trackers enable publishers to avoid this risk.

Third, CMP-providers can integrate different legal frameworks into the CMP and thus enable the CMP to adjust the cookie banner to the user's location dynamically. A CMP can, for example, use the location of a user to detect which privacy law applies—e.g., the GDPR or the CCPA—and can adjust the request for consent (i.e., the cookie banner) accordingly. In doing so, the CMP can help the publisher to comply with privacy regulations worldwide.

6.1.2 Use of Consent Management Platform (CMP) for Managing Permission

In addition to supporting publishers in requesting permission, the CMP provides the technology to store, in a structured manner, information about a user's decisions in response to permission requests, alongside information about the cookie banner variant to which the user was exposed. This structured storage facilitates the process of managing the user's permissions in several ways.

First, it enables the publisher to easily exchange information about the user's permissions with other involved parties. If, for example, publisher A uses the service of firm B for the analysis of individual click-through rates, then firm B acts as a data processor on behalf of publisher A. Firm B is only allowed to analyze the data if the user explicitly consented to this activity. Therefore, publisher A and firm B need to exchange information about the user's permissions regarding personal data processing.

Second, the structured storage inherent to the CMP provides a technological interface for the user to update or retract permission. By law, the user has the right to retract permission for data processing at any point in time. Therefore, many CMPs enable the publisher to embed a link on its website that opens the cookie banner again (in many cases, this link directs the user to the second layer of the cookie banner), or that activates a user interface that offers the possibility to alter permissions for data processing. Figure 13, for example, outlines the implementation of such a link on the website of Bloomberg Europe. The link opens the second layer of the cookie banner of the website directly.

Figure 13: *Managing Cookie Settings at Bloomberg.com*

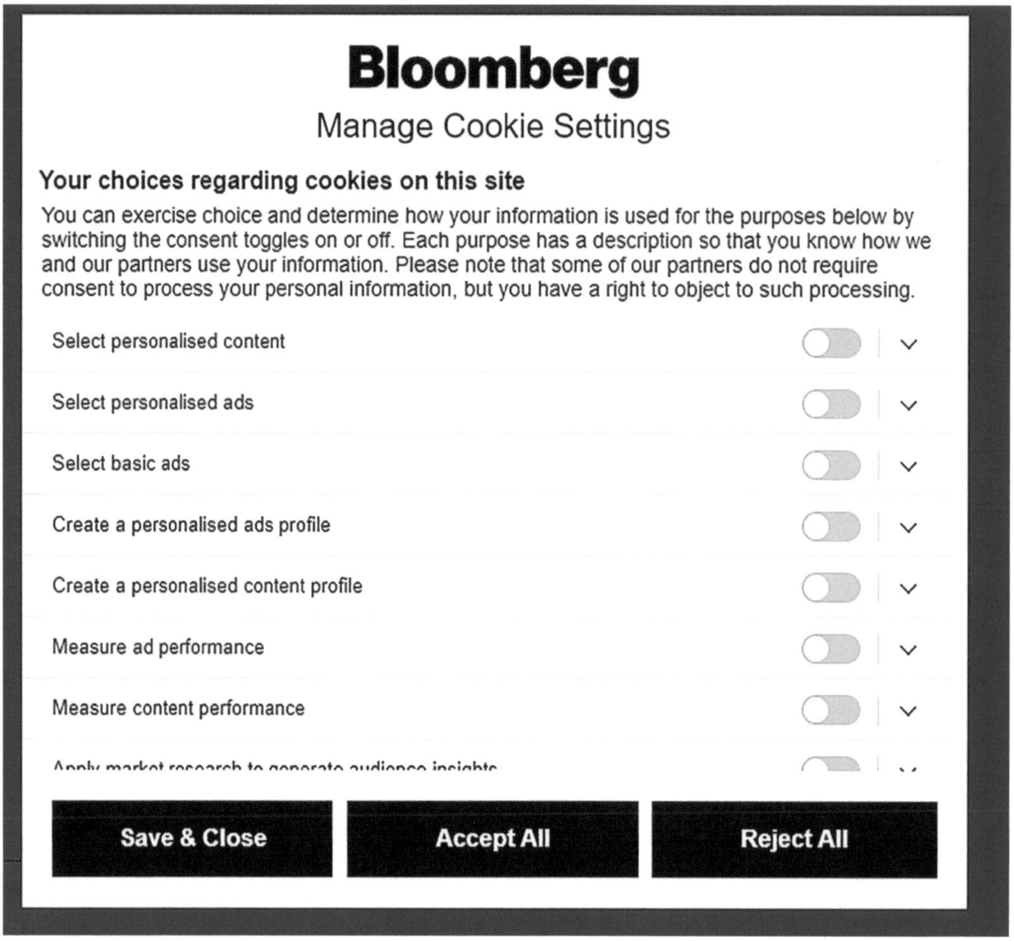

A third means by which the CMP facilitates consent management is by creating a so-called "consent log" containing a history of all events related to the user's permission decisions—including the initial decision and subsequent changes. Such a consent log is helpful in documenting and retracing the history of a user's decisions with regard to consent (Figure 14). An entry to such a log file consists of at least three elements:

- an identifier, such as an anonymized IP address,
- a time-stamp, and
- the activity that the user performed, such as selecting the "accept all" option on the cookie banner.

Figure 14: *Example of a History of a User's Decisions on Permission for Personal Data Processing*

Source: www.didomi.io/de/plattform/berichten-kontrollieren

This consent log offers several benefits. First, it provides the publisher with proof of its legal basis for data processing—i.e., the user's consent—if needed, for example, for compliance audit purposes. Second, it allows the publisher to analyze when a user gave or retracted permission for various data processing activities. For example, a user might provide publisher A with consent for behavioral targeting for advertising and retract the consent for behavioral targeting at a later point in time. Combining data from the consent log file with data about delivered ads could then help the publisher understand which advertising might have led to the retraction of consent.

6.2 Software for the User

The user's challenge when browsing online is to decide on and respond to each web-site's initial request for permission, keep track of all decisions and update the decisions if desired. Researchers from academia and industry started to develop, often in cooperation, so-called "Personal Information Management Services" (PIMS). The underlying vision of most PIMS is the provision of a tool that centralizes all information regarding a user's data and enables the user to manage in- and outflow of the user's data in one place. The scope of these PIMS is usually beyond mere consent decisions and often includes all sorts of data, including data from social media such as Instagram, LinkedIn or Twitter.

Many PIMS aim at automatically detecting and responding to data requests, such as consent requests. In such a case, the user only needs to provide her privacy preferences once in the PIMS and update it if the privacy preferences of the user change. Such an update then automatically notifies and updates all other actors that process the user's data.

Automating requires synchronization between the user's PIMS and data controllers and data processors from the industry. This synchronization poses several challenges, such as establishing connections between all the involved actors and a common technical language. At this point, many technical and legal challenges persist, such as whether the PIMS should save the user's data in the cloud, which facilitates synchronization among actors, or locally on the user's device, which usually offers higher data security. Given the various challenges, most PIMS are still under development.

Currently, users mainly have access to a few tools providing a basic version of a PIMS and focusing on consent decisions. These tools are browser extensions, available free of charge, primarily for Google Chrome and Mozilla Firefox. Subsequently, we describe them in more detail.

6.2.1 Use of Browser Extensions for Making Decisions on Permission

The few browser extensions that assist the user in deciding on permissions for data processing either block cookie banners or automatically respond to requests for permission for personal data processing. Using a browser extension that blocks cookie banners means that the user does not grant permission for any data processing activities. In other words, legally, the user is a "deny all" user. On some websites, the user appears technically with an unanswered request for permission, which can interfere with website functionality.

Among browser extensions that respond automatically to cookie banners, some block all cookies, whereas others provide "minimal consent", i.e., they only allow first-party cookies that are required for the website to function (= "functional cookies"). A significant problem with these automatic responses is that specifications of consent differ widely across cookie banners. Some rely on the function that cookies fulfill (e.g., functional cookies, analytics cookies, marketing cookies), some use the Transparency and Consent Framework (TCF)—a framework developed by IAB Europe for obtaining consent (described in detail in Section 7); and the rest use other specifications. Thus, even if a browser extension is informed of the user's preferences, it might not be able to respond appropriately to all websites' specifications.

A notable example of a very promising browser extension is the "advanced data protection control" (ADPC) browser extension, which offers advantages for publishers and users. ADPC is a joint project of the consumer protection agency NOYB (Section 9.4.1) and the Sustainable Computing Lab at the Vienna University of Economics and Business. ADPC allows publishers to request permission either using the TCF or formulating specific permission requests, making ADPC interoperable with other systems. It allows users to set general signals, e.g., "object to all", to set specific signals, e.g., consent to a specific request, or to combine general and specific signals, e.g., "reject all, but consent to requests 'A' and 'D'". It allows users to either set global options that apply to all publishers or set publisher-specific preferences (www.dataprotectioncontrol.org). ADPC is still under development, and a prototype is available in the browser's web store. As of November 2021, ADPC has 145 Chrome users.

The most downloaded browser extension, "I don't care about cookies", sometimes accepts all and sometimes accepts only necessary cookies, depending on what is technologically easier to execute for the extension. The popularity of this browser extension (more than 600,000 downloads for Chrome as of November 2021) might indicate that many users prefer not to receive a cookie banner when visiting a website, and are willing to forgo the opportunity to make a differentiated decision regarding their permission preferences.

The use of these tools entails certain disadvantages. First, these tools begin to operate before a website loads, thereby increasing the site's loading time and, in some cases, even preventing loading altogether. These effects likely worsen the user's online experience.

Another concern is that some users might lack the technological sophistication needed to seek out these tools and install them. A lack of technological expertise among users could explain why the download numbers of the browser extensions are relatively low. Indeed, as of November 2021, most consent management-related browser extensions for Chrome have fewer than 1,000 downloads each. Only a few browser extensions—e.g., Consent-O-Matic or Consent Manager—have up to 10,000 downloads. The only browser extension with a truly substantial number of downloads is "I don't care about cookies", mentioned above—yet the 600,000 users who downloaded this extension are still a relatively meager group, given that the EU has about 400 million Internet users, and Chrome has a market share in Europe of 60%.

6.2.2 Use of Browser Extensions for Managing Permissions

For the user, managing permissions entails keeping track of each decision made to grant a website permission for data processing. A basic tool for this purpose would list all permissions that the user provided. However, to the best of our knowledge, no browser extension or other tool exists to provide this service. Some browser extensions support the user in making initial permission decisions and document websites where the user blocked cookies or cookie banners. Major web browsers keep a record of installed cookies that users can access, enabling users to delete all or certain cookies.

With the development of PIMS, we will likely see such tools in the future. Sophisticated versions could also enable the user to request information about the data stored on a particular website (Section 4.3.1) and request the deletion of the data.

6.3 Main Takeaways

The main takeaways from Section 6 are:

- CMPs help actors in the online advertising industry obtain and manage user permissions, towards supplying a legal basis for personal data processing.
- CMP-providers provide publishers with services, alongside several additional benefits (e.g., cookie banner optimization), and have thus emerged as a new and important actor in the online advertising industry.
- Only a few tools are currently available that help users make and manage decisions on permissions. These tools have certain disadvantages, including increasing page loading time, and some even conflict with website functionality.

7

Getting User Permission for Personal Data Processing via the Transparency and Consent Framework (TCF)

In this section, we delve further into the practical challenges that firms in the advertising industry face in supplying a GDPR-compliant legal basis for their data processing activities. In particular, this section elaborates on the Transparency and Consent Framework (TCF), an industry initiative launched by IAB Europe for assisting firms in addressing the challenges for getting user permission. We note that, in practice, the process of ensuring the GDPR compliance is similar for the two legal bases that are applicable to the advertising industry, namely, (i) a user's explicit consent, or (ii) legitimate interest for processing data (see Section 4.5 for a detailed discussion of these legal bases). In both cases, the firm must get the user's permission for data processing, with the difference being that reliance on consent requires the user to opt-in to data processing, whereas reliance on legitimate interest requires the user not to opt-out. For convenience and for clarity of presentation, in what follows, we generally address consent and non-objection to legitimate interest simultaneously, using the term "permission" to refer to both of these concepts.

7.1 Challenges of Getting Permission

To get a user's permission for personal data processing, a firm has to take the following three steps: (1) specifying the purposes of data processing for which permission is being provided (Section 4.4.4); (2) handling the permission—which includes both asking for permission and storing permission; and (3) checking the permission for data transfer, i.e., verifying that any transfer of data to other firms is carried out in accordance with the permissions that the user has provided. A firm faces challenges in each step. Table 8 provides an overview of the three steps, the actions that each step entails, and the corresponding challenges, which we discuss in detail in what follows. Note that in Table 8 and throughout this section, we use the term "vendors" to refer to other actors (see Section 2.4), in accordance with the terminology used by the TCF.

Table 8: *Steps, Actions, and Challenges in Getting User Permission for Personal Data Processing towards Supplying a Legal Basis under the GDPR*

Steps	Actions	Challenges	
Step 1: Specify Purposes for Permission	Define specified, explicit, and legitimate purposes for which to get permission for	Specify purposes to get permission that are a. Accurate b. Explicit c. Convenient to communicate with users and other firms	
Step 2: Handle Permission	Ask for user's permission	a. Design and run cookie banners b. Publishers ask for permission on behalf of several vendors with heterogeneous purposes	Combine asking for and storing permission
	Store user's permission	Store user's permission in a way that a. Takes small storage space b. Lowers the cost of vendors to access and read stored permission	
Step 3: Check Permission for Data Transfer	Data sending firms check whether data receiving firms have the permissions	Ensure that data sending and receiving firms have permission for identical purposes before data transfer a. From publishers to vendors b. From vendors to vendors	

7.1.1 Challenges of Specifying Purposes for Permission

Step 1 ("specifying purposes for permission") describes how a firm tries to comply with Article 5 para. 1 point (b) of the GDPR: "Personal data shall be collected for specified, explicit and legitimate purposes." In other words, in this step, the firm must identify legitimate purposes for using the processed data and specify these purposes in a clear (explicit) manner. Moreover, according to Article 13 para. 1 of the GDPR, a firm needs to communicate the specified purposes with its users. Notably, it must specify and communicate the purposes of data collection not only on its own behalf but also on behalf of all firms to which it transfers users' personal data, and it must also identify these firms (Article 13, para. 1, point e): "the data controller shall [inform the data subject about] the recipients or categories of recipients of the personal data, if any."

The GDPR itself does not define which "specified, explicit and legitimate purposes" are acceptable, leaving room for interpretation. Consequently, it is possible that ten different firms will come up with ten different ways to specify their purposes. For example, Firm A might specify and label two purposes: (1) cookies for payment information; (2) tracking users' behavior online. Meanwhile, Firm B might specify the same two purposes but label them differently from Firm A: (1) cookies to process payment; (2) cookies monitoring users online. If these two firms were to collaborate, the two different labels would make it challenging to match these two purposes automatically—though the purposes are effectively identical. In addition, the specifications can also differ substantially. Thus, the potential for heterogeneity in purpose specification makes communication to users and between firms challenging.

In light of the above, we suggest that firms face three major challenges in the step of specifying purposes for data processing activities (Table 8): namely, specifying purposes in a manner that is (1) accurate, (2) explicit, and (3) convenient to communicate with users and other firms.

Challenge 1: Accuracy. In order to achieve accuracy, a firm must specify the purposes of data collection in a manner that is both GDPR-compliant and commonly accepted, thereby reducing the likelihood of misunderstanding. Achieving accuracy is challenging because the definitions and rules in the GDPR (Section 4) are abstract and open to interpretation. Indeed, there are disparities in interpreting the GDPR compliance among the Data Protection Authorities themselves. For example, the Data Protection Authorities of the UK and Spain require that analytic cookies get consent, while Germany disagrees, and France as well as Italy allows for several exceptions (Voisin et al. 2019). Hence, it is difficult for a firm to find a GDPR-compliant specification that is robust to all interpretations.

Another aspect that makes accuracy challenging is the possibility of heterogeneous specifications of similar purposes, as in our previous example of Firm A and Firm B. Suppose that Firm A transfers data to Firm B. In order for this transfer to take place, both firms must ensure that they have user permission for the two purposes specified by Firm B. Due to the different labels, Firm B may find it challenging to decide whether the purposes specified by Firm A accurately match its own specified purposes.

Challenge 2: Explicitness. The GDPR requires that a firm's data collection activities be made explicit, i.e., fully transparent to the user. However, the GDPR does not indicate the exact information that firms must provide in order to achieve sufficient explicitness. Accordingly, firms face the challenge of identifying which information will provide users and other firms with a sense of explicitness.

Challenge 3: Convenient Communication. Convenient communication entails using wording that reduces the chances of misunderstanding, while remaining concise and easily accessible to users and other firms. Again, because the GDPR does not specify which wordings should be used to describe the various purposes of data collection, it is challenging for a firm to identify the optimal wordings in this regard. In particular, firms may face a trade-off between using more words to achieve accuracy and making the text concise and accessible (Kulyk et al. 2020).

7.1.2 Challenges of Handling Permission

As shown in Table 8, step 2 of getting permission ("handling permission") consists of two actions: asking for user permission and storing user permission. We note that Section 5 provides additional discussion of these actions alongside the costs that they might inflict on firms and on users, and Section 5 provides information on technological tools used to mitigate these costs.

Action 1: Asking for Permission. This action involves a publisher asking for the user's permission to have her data processed for the purposes that the publisher has specified. A publisher relies on a cookie banner to ask for the user's permission (Section 5). A user's positive response to the publisher's request implies that the publisher has obtained permission to process the user's personal data.

As discussed in previous sections, asking for user permission can be challenging for a publisher because designing and running a cookie banner on web pages requires technical knowledge that some firms lack (Section 5.1.1.1). Moreover, a publisher must ask for permission on behalf of all the vendors to which it transfers user data for processing, as these vendors do not have direct access to the user. It may be challenging for a publisher to centralize its vendors' heterogeneous requests for permission, as different vendors may have different specifications for purposes (as discussed in Section 7.1.1).

Action 2: Storing Permission. After asking a user for permission, the publisher must locally store information about the user's response—namely, whether the user has given permission for each specific purpose corresponding to each vendor. By storing this information, the publisher can avoid re-requesting the user's consent each time the user visits its website.

Storing permission can be challenging in two ways. First, the publisher has to find a way to encode and store the users' decisions in a small amount of space. Indeed, a user's granular decisions on permissions can form massive amounts of information. Publishers pass this information via HTTP requests throughout the chain of data transfer. Since there is a size limit for such requests, a publisher has to store permission information compactly.

Second, it is challenging to store permission information in a way that enables vendors to access and read the information in a manner that is not excessively costly. Indeed, a vendor may incur high costs to access stored permission information, particularly when it transfers such information to other vendors. Recall that a vendor has to rely on a publisher to ask for permission on its behalf. Suppose Vendor A transfers data to Vendor B; Vendor A has to access the publisher's permission information to see whether Vendor B has received user permission. This process can become costly if Vendor A transfers data to many other vendors (Figure 5) and has to contact the publisher repeatedly. In addition, if a vendor works with multiple publishers that store information in different ways, it incurs costs associated with reading various storage formats.

Aside from the challenges outlined above, publishers face challenges in keeping stored permissions up to date. In effect, these challenges relate to the need to integrate the action of asking for permission with the action of storing permission. Suppose a user updates her permission settings and revokes permission that she granted in the past for a particular purpose. The publisher needs to update the permission information for each actor, and to ensure that all involved actors have the same, current information at the same point in time. To achieve this goal, it is necessary to integrate cookie banners with storage and data processing systems. Such integration poses both technical and legal challenges to firms. Specifically, a firm needs an information technology expert to execute the technical aspects of the integration, and it also needs a lawyer—one who is also comfortable with information technology—to verify that the procedure is compliant with the GDPR. Such interdisciplinary talents are rare and expensive to hire.

7.1.3 Challenges of Checking Permission for Data Transfer

Step 3 ("check permission for data transfer") describes the obligation for a firm that transfers data to other parties. Before Firm A (sender) transfers data to Firm B (receiver), Firm A has to identify Firm B's purposes for processing and verify that Firm B has permission to process the user's data for these purposes.

Carrying out this action is challenging. As discussed in Section 7.1.1, the GDPR offers firms the flexibility to specify their own purposes for data processing, and different firms may specify similar purposes in different ways. This diversity in specification increases the time and effort involved in the collaboration between firms. Furthermore, it may be challenging for both firms to argue that their purposes are indeed identical.

This challenge is further complicated by the specific roles fulfilled by the firms involved in the data transfer. For example, in a publisher-to-vendor data transfer, a publisher has to handle user permission on behalf of a vendor, and then check whether the permission it has obtained is indeed applicable to the purposes that the vendor has specified. This procedure, entailing multiple responsibilities imposed by the GDPR, is highly complicated. Similarly, in a vendor-to-vendor data transfer, the data-sending vendor always has to check with the publisher whether the data-receiving vendor has user permission. This process can entail substantial effort, particularly when the vendor collaborates with many other vendors, as illustrated in Figure 5.

7.2 Transparency and Consent Framework (TCF)

On April 25, 2018, IAB Europe launched the TCF as a means of tackling the challenges discussed in Section 7.1. It launched an updated version of the TCF, TCF 2.0, in August 2019. The TCF is an industry initiative, aiming at providing a solution to get user permission with guidelines and tools. In order to adopt the solution, a firm has to register with IAB Europe, denoted as participating in TCF in the following sections. The TCF was formulated on the basis of extensive consultation with representatives from different fields in the online advertising industry—including technology vendors (Xandr), CMPs (OneTrust), and publishers (The Telegraph).

Specifically, the TCF aims to introduce a standard that

- creates a standardized terminology of purposes shared by all participants;
- provides tools to facilitate asking for permission (Global Vendor List) and storing permission (Transparency and Consent String); and
- creates a procedure to check permissions for processing personal data before transferring user data between firms.

Note that each bullet point corresponds to one of the three steps described in the previous section, and summarized in Table 8: specifying purposes for permission, handling permission, and checking permission for data transfer.

In what follows, we provide a step-by-step explanation of how, in practice, a firm can use the TCF to execute each of the three steps and overcome the associated challenges. The TCF was envisioned as a well-documented and accepted standard that should help firms to comply with the GDPR. A Canadian initiative (www.iabcanada.com/transparency-and-consent-framework) builds upon the idea of the European initiative. Yet, the Irish Council for Civil Liberties suspects that the TCF infringes the GDPR. We will discuss their concerns in more detail in Section 9.4.2.

7.3 Mitigating Challenges in Specifying Purposes for Permission

The first step in getting permission for personal data processing is to specify the purposes for such processing. As noted in Section 7.1.1, the main challenges a firm faces in this step include formulating the specifications in a manner that is accurate, explicit, and convenient to communicate with users and other firms. To mitigate these challenges, the TCF provides a list of Purposes, Special Purposes, Features, Special Features, and Stacks. We elaborate on each of these concepts in what follows.

7.3.1 Facilitating Accuracy of Communication

7.3.1.1 Purposes

As pointed out in Section 7.1.1, as the GDPR does not define precisely what a "specified, explicit and legitimate purpose" is, a firm may find it difficult to specify purposes that are GDPR-compliant under the interpretations of all parties, as well as to match its own purposes to those of other firms (in the case of data transfer between firms).

To overcome these challenges, the TCF proposes ten specific purposes, which are shown in Table 9.

Table 9: *Specification of Purposes in the Transparency and Consent Framework (TCF) 2.0*

Name of Purpose	Specification
Purpose 1	Store and/ or access information on a device
Purpose 2	Select basic ads
Purpose 3	Create a personalized ads profile
Purpose 4	Select personalized ads
Purpose 5	Create a personalized content profile
Purpose 6	Select personalized content
Purpose 7	Measure ad performance
Purpose 8	Measure content performance
Purpose 9	Apply market research to generate audience insights
Purpose 10	Develop and improve products

TCF uses the term "Purpose" to refer to each of the ten purposes specified in Table 9. To avoid confusion, throughout the remainder of this section, we refer to "Purpose" specified by the TCF as a "TCF purpose" and refer to a specific TCF purpose (e.g., Purpose 2) as "Purpose N" where "N" is an integer from 1 to 10.

Seven of the ten TCF purposes relate to either advertisement (Purposes 2, 3, 4, and 7) or content (Purposes 5, 6, and 8). Moreover, the purpose specification structures for advertisement and for content are similar.

Notably, for Purposes 2–10, a firm can claim either consent or legitimate interest as the legal basis for data processing. For Purpose 1, however—which does not indicate a broader motivation for data processing but instead refers solely to the act of storing or accessing information on a device—a firm cannot claim legitimate interest and must obtain explicit consent. The motivation for including Purpose 1 in the list of TCF purposes is that it corresponds to the obligation of Article 5 (3) of the ePrivacy Directive (relevant for the "Planet49" decision of the European Court of Justice). Article 5 (3) emphasizes the importance of getting user consent for storing information.

Purpose 1 is unique because data controllers cannot pursue Purpose 1 on its own but rather only in conjunction with another TCF purpose, which is an unavoidable logical outcome. For example, if Google wishes to display an ad to a user—whether personalized (Purpose 4) or non-personalized (Purpose 2)—it must obtain consent for Purpose

1. If the user denies consent for Purpose 1 but accepts consent for Purpose 4 and Purpose 2, Google will still drop the ad request and serve no ad, regardless of whether the ad is personalized or not (Roth 2020). The reason is that Google relies on cookies or mobile identifiers for both non-personalized ads (e.g., for frequency capping or fraud detection) and personalized ads (targeting). The example of Google further highlights the importance of Purpose 1. Note that data processors might still need Purpose 1 but not any of the other TCF purposes because they rely on the legal bases established by their data controllers. Moreover, data controllers may also declare one or more Purposes 2-10, without declaring Purpose 1 if they do not need access to the device.

With the help of the ten TCF purposes, all firms using TCF can communicate accurately with one another. For example, when a firm mentions Purpose 4, every other firm knows that the firm is referring to "selecting personalized ads."

We note that the specifications outlined in Table 9, corresponding to ten TCF purposes, reflect TCF 2.0, which launched in August 2019. TCF 1.0 (launched in April 2018) contained only five purposes. TCF 2.0 made the purposes more granular, in accordance with the WP259 guideline on consent (European Data Protection Board 2020). The guideline points out that granularity is an element of valid consent. This adjustment to conform to legal guidelines reflects that the TCF has been improving and revising its purpose specifications.

7.3.1.2 Special Purposes

In addition to the ten TCF purposes outlined above, the TCF specifies two Special Purposes, defined as purposes that firms must fulfill in order to technically be able to serve ads. Table 10 contains the two Special Purposes stipulated in TCF 2.0. Legitimate interest is the only legal basis that is applicable to these Special Purposes, and users cannot execute the "Right to Object" to these legitimate interests (Article 21, GDPR). The reasons are the following. Special Purpose 1 refers to a firm's legal responsibilities, so a firm must be allowed to pursue the purpose. Special Purpose 2 is technically necessary for delivering information over the network to an IP address. Although the "Right to Object" to Special Purposes is not technically supported by the TCF, publishers and their partner vendors can still establish some signaling mechanism to enable the execution of the "Right to Object".

Table 10: *Specification of Special Purposes in the Transparency and Consent Framework (TCF) 2.0*

Name	Specification
Special Purpose 1	Ensure security, prevent fraud, and debug
Special Purpose 2	Technically deliver ads or content

7.3.2 Facilitating Explicitness of Communication

7.3.2.1 Features

The TCF further specifies several Features. Features are not purposes in themselves. They are methods to process data related to one or more TCF purposes. Features are technically necessary to achieve certain TCF purposes; once the user has given permission for a particular TCF purpose, she does not need to provide additional permission for the associated Features. Note that a Feature is always linked to a TCF purpose and if there is no legal basis supporting that TCF purpose, the Feature has no meaning. Features require no legal basis, and information about them is provided to the user solely as a means of improving communication explicitness, that is, to provide the user with information about the methods that firms will apply to the user's data to achieve the approved (Special) Purposes. Table 11 contains the content of the Features.

Table 11: *Specification of Features in the Transparency and Consent Framework (TCF) 2.0*

Name	Specification
Feature 1	Match and combine offline data sources
Feature 2	Link different devices
Feature 3	Receive and use automatically-sent device characteristics for identification

7.3.2.2 Special Features

Apart from Features, the TCF also contains Special Features. Special Features are similar to Features because firms may use them as a technical means of implementing one or more TCF purposes. However, Special Features are more privacy intrusive than Features are (e.g., precise geolocation), meaning that they relate to processing of data that may be more sensitive to a user. Therefore, a firm can only use the Special Features with consent as a legal basis. Table 12 shows the two Special Features.

Table 12: *Specification of Special Features in the Transparency and Consent Framework (TCF) 2.0*

Name	Specification
Special Feature 1	Use precise geolocation data
Special Feature 2	Actively scan device characteristics for identification

Figure 15 summarizes the differences in legal bases for Purposes, Special Purposes, Features, and Special Features in TCF. A green cell indicates that a particular legal basis (column) is applicable to a particular (Special) Purpose or (Special) Feature (row). In almost all cases in which a particular legal basis applies, the user has the right to make a decision, i.e., to provide/deny consent, or to accept/object to the legitimate interest. The only exception is for Special Purposes, which are grounded in the legal basis of legitimate interest, and to which the user cannot object.

Figure 15: *Legal Bases for (Special) Purposes and (Special) Features in the Transparency and Consent Framework (TCF) 2.0*

	Legal Basis	
	Consent	**Legitimate Interest**
Purposes		
Users can opt-in or opt-out for Purpose 2 to Purpose 10		
1 Store and/or access information on a device	Yes	No
2 Select basic ads	Yes	Yes
3 Create a personalized ads profile	Yes	Yes
4 Select personalized ads	Yes	Yes
5 Create a personalized content profile	Yes	Yes
6 Select personalized content	Yes	Yes
7 Measure ad performance	Yes	Yes
8 Measure content performance	Yes	Yes
9 Apply market research to generate audience insights	Yes	Yes
10 Develop and improve products	Yes	Yes
Special Purposes		
Users cannot opt-out of the Special Purposes		
1 Ensure security, prevent fraud and debug	No	Yes
2 Technically deliver ads or content	No	Yes
Features		
Users cannot make decisions for the Features		
1 Match and combine offline data sources	No	No
2 Link different devices	No	No
3 Receive and use automatically-sent device characteristics for identification	No	No
Special Features		
Users can opt-in for the Special Features		
1 Use precise geolocation data	Yes	No
2 Actively scan device characteristics for identification	Yes	No

7.3.3 Facilitating Convenience of Communication with Stacks

To provide firms with a simplified way to ask for permission, requiring users to make fewer decisions without sacrificing granular information or choices, TCF proposes Stacks—pre-defined groups of TCF purposes and/or Special Features. The TCF 2.0 Policy defines 42 Stacks that a publisher can choose to display on its cookie banner. Table 13 provides an example of a TCF Stack, labeled as Stack 2. If a publisher uses Stack 2, the publisher displays the name of the Stack "Basic ads and ad measurement" in the first layer of the User Interface (UI). The publisher usually displays the Stack description and corresponding TCF in a further layer, e.g., on a separate page. By choosing "Yes" for this Stack, a user simultaneously gives consent to Purpose 2 and to Purpose 7. As indicated by some DPAs (e.g., CNIL in France), displaying Stacks instead of TCF purposes improves the convenience of communication between the publisher and the user because the user has to make fewer decisions (just one instead of two decisions in the Stack 2 example). Nevertheless, the TCF still requires publishers to enable granular choices for each TCF purpose. Part of the convenience brought by the TCF might also be that users get progressively used to semi-standardized interfaces and standardized terminology so that they are increasingly efficient in making their choices over time.

Table 13: *Example of a Stack in the Transparency and Consent Framework (TCF) 2.0*

Stack Number	2
Name	Basic ads and ad measurement
Description	Basic ads can be served. Ad performance can be measured.
Purposes included	Purpose 2: Select basic ads
	Purpose 7: Measure ad performance

Note that different Stacks may contain overlapping TCF purposes. When selecting from the pool of 42 Stacks, a publisher cannot choose Stacks with the same TCF purpose. For example, Stack 2 contains Purposes 2 and 7; Stack 3 contains Purposes 2, 3, and 4. A publisher cannot include Stack 2 and Stack 3 simultaneously, as both Stacks include Purpose 2. If a publisher were to include both Stacks, it might obtain conflicting responses from users, e.g., if a user accepts Stack 2 but denies permission for Stack 3. For the same reason, a publisher cannot present a particular TCF purpose both as part of a Stack and outside of a Stack simultaneously.

To sum up, the TCF assists firms in overcoming the challenges associated with specifying purposes for personal data processing. Specifically, it enhances (i) accuracy of specification—by providing a standardized, clearly defined, and granular set of (Special) Purposes; (ii) explicitness—by providing clear descriptions of (Special) Features that are technically necessary for the fulfillment of the specified Purposes; and (iii) convenience of communication—by creating groups of TCF purposes and/or Special Features, called Stacks, which are presented concisely and that enable users to make decisions on multiple TCF purposes simultaneously. Furthermore, the TCF is very clear about the applicable legal basis and possible user decisions for each scenario.

7.4 Mitigating Challenges in Handling Permission

The second step in getting permission for personal data processing is handling permission, via (1) asking for permission, and (2) storing permission. There are several challenges a firm faces in these actions (Table 8). The TCF provides tools to mitigate the challenges, which we will introduce in this section.

7.4.1 Facilitating Asking for Permission

7.4.1.1 Global Vendor List (GVL)

The requirements that a firm must fulfill under the TCF in order to handle permission for data processing vary depending on whether the firm is a publisher (Section 2.1) or a vendor (Section 2.4). The critical difference between a publisher and a vendor in handling permission is that a publisher has direct contact with a user and asks for permission on its own, whereas a vendor has no direct contact with a user and needs to rely on a publisher to ask for user permission on the vendor's behalf.

Section 7.1.2 points out that asking for permission is challenging. To obtain permission, a vendor must tell its partner publishers the purposes for which it requires such permission. As a publisher cooperates with many vendors, a publisher has to centralize all the vendors' requests for permission. The heterogeneity of vendors and their respective requests makes centralizing vendor permission challenging. Within the TCF, vendors disclose their required purposes uniformly via a registration process. The standardized registration process and the standardized purpose specification introduced in Section 7.3 simplify the challenge of centralizing vendor permission requests.

To register with the TCF, a vendor must have a sufficient reputation (e.g., be a member in good standing with some industry associations) and pay an annual fee of 1500€. A vendor who registers with the TCF discloses which of the TCF-specified (Special) Purposes and (Special) Features (Table 9 - Table 12) it pursues. At the same time, the vendor also decides which legal basis to use for each of these (Special) Purposes and (Special) Features. When declaring legitimate interest as the legal basis in the GVL, vendors have to attest that they have carried out adequate Legitimate Interests Assessments (LIA) that operate a balancing between user and vendor interests. IAB Europe provides guidance on how to do this.

After receiving the registration application of a vendor, IAB Europe verifies the vendor's identity and the vendor's ability to maintain its service while sticking to TCF regulations. Approved vendors appear on the Global Vendor List (GVL) (www.iabeurope.eu/vendor-list-tcf-v2-0). The GVL is a list of TCF-registered vendors and the respective (Special) Purposes and (Special) Features each vendor uses. The GVL is publicly available via its official website and updated weekly, enhancing each vendor's data processing transparency.

Note that the verification process conducted by IAB Europe provides no warranty of GDPR compliance. In other words, the TCF does not certify that its approved vendors are entirely GDPR-compliant.

From the GVL, a publisher knows what TCF purposes each vendor pursues, and with which legal basis. Then, a publisher chooses the vendors it intends to collaborate with from the GVL (hereafter referred to as partner vendors). By default, the purposes that each vendor pursues according to the GVL apply to all publishers. If a publisher prefers a legal basis for a specific TCF purpose that is different from the one specified by a particular vendor, the publisher can use Publisher Restrictions to modify the way they collaborate. For example, if a particular vendor uses legitimate interest for Purpose 3, a publisher can restrict the TCF purpose and require consent. In this way, a publisher and a vendor can collaborate more flexibly.

If a vendor changes the (Special) Purposes and (Special) Features it uses, it needs to update its information provided to IAB Europe. These updates are included in the next weekly update of GVL. By being connected to the GVL, all publishers automatically have access to the most recent version available via their CMPs (which are also registered with the TCF; see Section 7.4.1.2). Yet, suppose the update requires more permissions, because of an additional (Special) Purposes and (Special) Features, an additional vendor, or a change of the legal basis from legitimate interest to consent. In that case, the publisher needs to ask all users again for their permission.

To sum up, TCF's registration process and the GVL standardize how a vendor discloses its purposes to publishers. Furthermore, the process and the GVL provide an efficient means for publishers to centralize and manage permissions for their partner vendors.

7.4.1.2 Consent Management Platforms (CMPs) Registered with the TCF

To ask for user permission, a publisher needs to equip its website with a cookie banner. As a firm faces technical challenges in designing and running a cookie banner (Section 7.1.1), a publisher relies on a CMP (Section 6.1) that registers with the TCF to assist in designing and running a cookie banner. Like a vendor, a CMP also has to submit a registration application to the TCF and pay an annual fee of 1500€. IAB Europe verifies whether the technical operation of a CMP is compliant with TCF regulations. Again, passing the verification does not guarantee complete GDPR compliance for a CMP. If a publisher participates in the TCF, it must use a CMP from the publicly available list of TCF-registered CMPs. A publisher can use a commercial CMP service or register its own (private) CMP. As of November 2021, there are 170 registered CMPs in the TCF. 53 (31%) of them are private CMPs.

A TCF-registered CMP provides technical support to design and run a cookie banner. More importantly, only TCF-registered CMPs can create, update and store the Transparency and Consent String, a tool to store consent, which we will introduce in the following subsection.

TCF-registered CMPs must follow the TCF guidelines. IAB Europe randomly audits CMPs for proper TCF implementation on publishers' websites and can admonish the CMP if violations occur. After three warnings, TCF can suspend a CMP, which means that all the publishers can no longer use the suspended CMP. Thus, IAB Europe creates a strong incentive for CMPs to ensure that the publishers correctly implement TCF when using their service.

7.4.2 Facilitating Storing Permission with Transparency and Consent String (TC String)

Storing consent for a user is technically challenging for two reasons. First, there is a lot of information to store. For example, for each purpose of each vendor, a user can decide whether to provide permission for that purpose or not. Second, publishers have to store permission information in a manner that enables vendors to access and read the stored information easily. The TCF created the Transparency and Consent string (TC string) to cope with these two problems.

The TC string is a piece of encoded character string capturing and storing all information about a user's permission decisions and other privacy preferences for a publisher. The TC string includes (1) (Special) Purposes and (Special) Features of each vendor cooperating with the publisher, (2) status of user permission (consent or non-objection to legitimate interest) to process data per purpose per vendor, (3) metadata and other restrictions (e.g., the time when the TC string was created).

Only TCF-registered CMPs can create and update a TC string. All information in the TC string is encoded in a space-efficient manner so as to enable the TC string to be passed between firms via HTTP GET requests with a storage limit. All publishers within the TCF use TC strings to store consent. All publishers and vendors rely on the Application Programming Interface (API) of a TCF-registered CMP to decode and read TC strings.

Thus, in effect, the TCF enables all firms to "speak the same language" when transmitting and reading information on user permissions (the TC string).

7.4.3 Integrating Asking for Permission and Storing Permission

Combining cookie banners, information storage, and data processing in a harmonized way is challenging because it involves technical knowledge from many fields. The TCF attempts to provide a standardized procedure to integrate these different fields, relying on the components described in previous sections (e.g., TCF specification of purposes, TCF tools to facilitate asking for and storing permission).

We describe this TCF procedure in detail with three representative cases summarized in Table 14. For these cases, we assume that one user visits a publisher five days in a row and once a day, and that consent is the legal basis for all pursued purposes. We arrange the cases from simple to complex in chronological order from Day 1 to Day 5.

Table 14: *Overview of Cases of Asking for and Storing Consent under the Transparency and Consent Framework (TCF)*

Case	Time	Actors	Consent for	Aim
Case 1	Day 1 Day 2	User X, Publisher A	Publisher A	The simplest case to understand how the TC string works
Case 2	Day 3 Day 4	User X, Publisher A, Vendor S (DSP)	Vendor S (DSP)	How a publisher asks for consent on behalf of its partner vendor
Case 3	Day 5	User X, Publisher A, Vendor S (DSP), Vendor P (ad exchange)	Vendor S (DSP) Vendor P (ad exchange)	How actors affect each other when having different consent statuses

Case 1 is a simple example to help understand how a TC string works. A publisher asks a user for consent on its own behalf and stores consent for the user. Case 2 is a general case describing how a publisher asks for and stores consent on behalf of its partner vendor. Case 3 is a case explaining how actors affect each other when having different consent statuses. For example, a vendor may lose access to a user's data if its partner vendor does not have the user's consent. To make the examples more intuitive, we use figures visualizing how consent information is asked for and stored.

7.4.3.1 Case 1: A Publisher Obtains Consent on its own Behalf

Case 1 captures the most straightforward case of collecting and storing consent, visualized in Figure 16. Day 1 describes what happens on the user's first visit to a publisher's website, and Day 2 depicts the user's second visit. On Day 1, User X visits Publisher A for the first time. Publisher A has no partner vendor, so it only needs user consent for itself to pursue its specified TCF purposes—in our example, Purpose 6 (select personalized content) and Purpose 8 (measure content performance) (Table 9).

Figure 16: *Process of Getting Consent under the Transparency and Consent Framework (TCF) for Case 1*

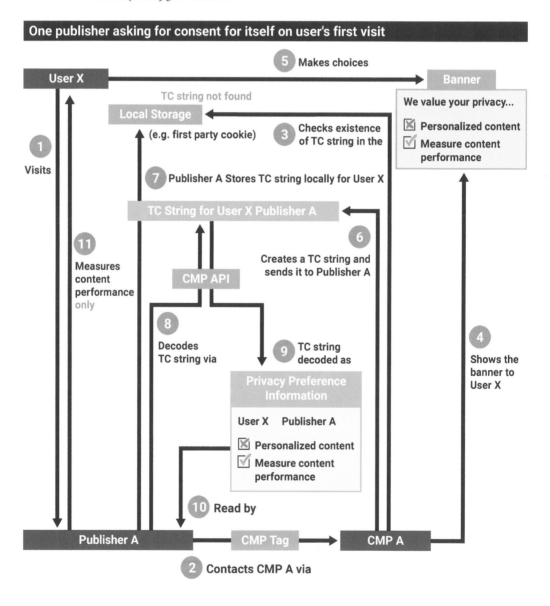

When User X arrives at the publisher's website (Step 1 in Figure 16), Publisher A contacts its CMP, CMP A, via a CMP tag, a JavaScript tag added to the website of Publisher A (Step 2). Then, the CMP code runs on the page and checks whether a TC string corresponding to Publisher A exists in User X's local storage (e.g., a first-party cookie) (Step 3). As this is User X's first visit to Publisher A, no such TC string is found. In such a case, CMP A shows a cookie banner on the website, e.g., as shown in Figure 10. The simplified cookie banner shown in Figure 16 (Step 4) lists out the two TCF purposes covered in our example: selecting personalized content and measuring content performance.

Next (Step 5 in Figure 16), User X makes choices on the cookie banner for each purpose, a "No" for personalized content and a "Yes" for performance measurement. Then, CMP A creates a TC string for User X–Publisher A by encoding the consent information according to the standard (Step 6). Publisher A stores the TC string locally on the device of User X (Step 7). In Step 8, Publisher A relies on its CMP API to decode the TC string. Then, Publisher A knows which purpose User X allows it to pursue, which we visualize in the yellow box of "Privacy Preference Information" in the center. Eventually, Publisher A can measure content performance based on User X's data but cannot provide any personalized content to User X.

On Day 2, User X visits the publisher for the second time. Steps 1-3 in Figure 16 remain unchanged. Assuming that User X has not deleted local storage since the previous visit, CMP A can detect the previously saved TC string and decode it for Publisher A. In other words, there is no need to show the cookie banner and go through Steps 4-7 again. As long as User X does not change consent information on the privacy policy page, Publisher A will rely on the stored consent information without re-obtaining permission. Overall, asking for and storing user consent in the simplest Case 1 is already a complicated procedure.

7.4.3.2 Case 2: A Publisher Obtains Consent on Behalf of a Vendor

Case 2, visualized in Figure 17, captures how a publisher asks for and stores consent on behalf of a vendor. Day 3 describes the first-visit example under the new assumptions, while Day 4 illustrates the second-visit example. On Day 3, Publisher A decides to offer ad slots on its website to monetize its content with ad revenue. Therefore, Publisher A chooses an ad tech vendor, Vendor S, from the GVL as its partner and notifies CMP A about this change. In this example, Vendor S is a Demand Side Platform (DSP) where a publisher lists its advertising inventory for advertisers to buy. Vendor S pursues two purposes with users' personal data: Purpose 2 (select basic ads) and Purpose 4 (select personalized ads) in Table 9.

Figure 17: *Process of Asking for and Storing Consent under the Transparency and Consent Framework (TCF) for Case 2*

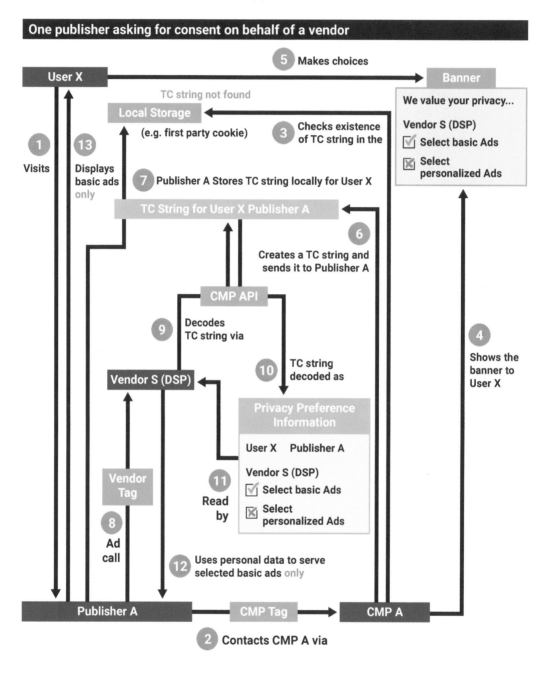

When User X visits Publisher A, the CMP tag code runs and checks whether a TC string with complete consent information exists. Although a TC string for Publisher A exists, the explicit consent is missing for Vendor S to process User X's data, as Vendor S has only recently been added. Thus, CMP A shows a new cookie banner to User X. The new cookie banner contains the TCF purposes for Vendor S and Publisher A. To make the illustration concise, we exclude the procedure of acquiring consent for Publisher A itself, which the Case 1 example has already described. User X sees Vendor S and its TCF purposes on the cookie banner and chooses a "Yes" for basic ad selection and a "No" for personalized ad selection. In Step 6, CMP A encodes the consent information into a new TC string for User X–Publisher A. Then, Publisher A saves the new TC string in the local storage of User X.

In Step 8, Publisher A signals Vendor S an ad call via a vendor tag. Before processing User X's data, Vendor S reads the TC string via the CMP API and knows that it can only use User X's data to select basic ads. Then, Vendor S serves basic ads to Publisher A for User X in Step 12.

On Day 4, User X visits Publisher A once more. In this scenario, similar to the scenario described for Day 2 (for Case 1), if User X has not deleted the TC string in the local storage, Publisher A and Vendor S can rely on the previously saved permissions as given. In other words, no cookie banner pops up, saving Steps 4-7.

7.4.3.3 Case 3: A Publisher Obtains Consent on Behalf of Multiple Vendors

Case 3, visualized in Figure 18, captures how a publisher asks for and stores consent on behalf of multiple vendors. Day 5 describes the first-visit example under the new assumptions. On Day 5, Publisher A starts to sell the ad slots via another ad tech vendor, Vendor P, an ad exchange. Thus, Vendor S (DSP) can now only buy ad slots via Vendor P (ad exchange). Both Vendor S and Vendor P use personal data to select basic (Purpose 2) ads and personalized ads (Purpose 4). Again, Publisher A informs CMP A about the recent addition of Vendor P and its TCF purposes.

Figure 18: *Process of Getting Consent under the Transparency and Consent Framework (TCF) for Case 3*

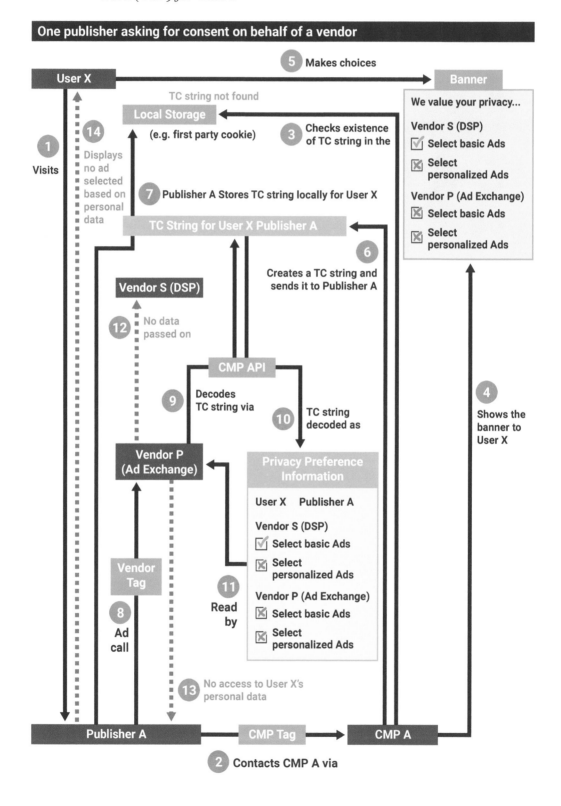

When User X visits Publisher A, Steps 1-3 occur again. As in the scenario described for Day 3 (Case 2), CMP A checks the local storage of User X and finds out that there are vendors and TCF purposes for which the user has not yet provided consent decisions. Therefore, CMP A shows a new cookie banner to User X with purposes and features for Publisher A, Vendor S, and Vendor P. We again neglect the procedures of asking for and storing consent for Publisher A itself for conciseness. Assume that User X ticks "Yes" for basic ad selection for Vendor S only, and "No" for the remaining TCF purposes, as displayed in the simplified banner in Figure 18. CMP A encodes the consent information into a new TC string, decoded and interpreted via the CMP API by Publisher A, Vendor S, and Vendor P.

When the vendor tag on the website runs in Step 8, Publisher A sends an ad call to Vendor P. However, Vendor P cannot use User X's data for either of the TCF purposes. Consequently, Vendor S has no access to the data, even though it has user consent for basic ad selection. The dashed grey arrow in Step 12 captures the loss of access to user data. This situation implies that, in Step 14, Vendor S can no longer show a basic ad that, according to the user's permission decisions, it would otherwise have been able to show for User X.

7.4.3.4 Example Procedures: Concluding Remarks

To keep our example simple and concise, we illustrated the elementary cases of a publisher obtaining consent only on its own behalf, for one vendor, or for two vendors. Even with our simplified focus, the procedures described were quite complex—Cases 2 and 3 even more so than Case 1. In reality, the complex interplay between publishers and vendors requires the technical solutions for these cases to be even more sophisticated than outlined. The TCF assists in mitigating this complexity by providing actors in the online advertising industry with clear procedures for integrating permission requests and permission storage.

Nevertheless, the current TCF procedure cannot take care of every connection in the complex interplay. For example, it is not strictly supervised whether vendors delete the received personal data when a user withdraws her consent or when she wants to have her personal data deleted.

7.5 Mitigating Challenges in Checking Permission for Data Transfer

The third step of getting permission for personal data processing is checking permission for data transfer, i.e., ensuring that data-sending and data-receiving firms have permission for identical purposes for transferring personal data—and that the permissions for each purpose correspond to identical legal bases (i.e., consent or legitimate interest). This procedure of matching purpose specifications and legal bases can be technically challenging. TCF attempts to mitigate these challenges by providing standardized checking and matching procedures, which we will introduce in what follows.

7.5.1 Facilitating Checking Permission for Publishers

In this section, we discuss the case where a publisher transfers data to other vendors. Recall that a vendor within the TCF discloses, through the GVL, which of the (Special) Purposes and (Special) Features (Table 9 - Table 12) it uses. A vendor also decides which legal basis to use to support each purpose it pursues. A vendor can only support Purpose 1 with consent. To support Purposes 2-10 (Table 9), a vendor has three options: (1) use only consent, (2) use only legitimate interest, (3) use either consent or legitimate interest. For the purposes supported by either consent or legitimate interest, a vendor sets a default legal basis. Then, it is the partner publisher who decides which legal basis to use for the vendor. Note that a firm can only use one legal basis to support one purpose.

More formally, for each purpose (Table 9) except for Purpose 1, a vendor has five options:

- Pursue the purpose and support with only consent as the legal basis.
- Pursue the purpose and support with only legitimate interest as the legal basis.
- Pursue the purpose and support with legitimate interest by default, but consent also feasible as the legal basis.
- Pursue the purpose and support with consent by default, but legitimate interest also feasible as the legal basis.
- Do not pursue the purpose.

Table 15 provides an example of the legal bases for the pursued TCF purposes of a specific vendor (Emerse Sverige AB), who pursues Purposes 1–9 and does not pursue Purpose 10. The vendor uses only consent to support Purpose 1, Purpose 3, and Purpose 4. The vendor uses only legitimate interest to support Purpose 7 and Purpose 8. The vendor uses either consent or legitimate interest to support Purpose 2 and Purpose 9, and in both cases the default legal basis is legitimate interest.

Table 15: *Legal Bases for Purposes under TCF Specification of an Example Vendor (here: Emerse Sverige AB)*

Vendor ID		8
Vendor Name		Emerse Sverige AB
Purpose ID	Purpose supported by only consent	Purpose 1
		Purpose 3
		Purpose 4
	Purpose supported by only legitimate interest	Purpose 7
		Purpose 8
	Purpose supported by legitimate interest by default, consent also feasible	Purpose 2
		Purpose 9
	Purpose supported by consent by default, legitimate interest also feasible	NA

Notes: Information from Global Vendor List Version 96 (2021 June)

A publisher has three options for the vendor for each purpose:

- Desire the vendor to pursue the purpose and support with consent as the legal basis.
- Desire the vendor to pursue the purpose and support with legitimate interest as the legal basis.
- Desire the vendor not to pursue the purpose.

Given that a publisher has requested permission for data processing on the vendor's behalf for a particular purpose, there are four options for the decision that a user can make:

In cases in which consent serves as the legal basis:

- Give consent to process data for the purpose (accept consent).
- Do not give consent to process data for the purpose (deny consent).

In cases in which legitimate interest serves as the legal basis:

- Accept legitimate interest to process data for the purpose (accept legitimate interest).
- Execute the "Right to Object" to legitimate interest to process data for the purpose (deny legitimate interest).

Thus, given that a publisher has a relationship with a vendor (i.e., intends to transfer user data to the vendor in accordance with TCF procedures), and given a particular TCF purpose, various outcomes can be obtained with regard to data transfer for that purpose. The outcome depends on the combination of (1) the option selected by the vendor, (2) the option selected by the publisher, and (3) the user's decision, given the option selected by the publisher. In particular, seven outcomes are possible (see Figure 19); we classify these outcomes into "Deal" and "No Deal." "Deal" means that a user's personal data are ultimately transferred for processing, while "No Deal" means that neither data transfer nor data processing takes place. The seven outcomes are as follows:

- Deal to transfer data upon consent.
- Deal to transfer data upon legitimate interest.
- No deal due to mismatched legal basis.
- No deal due to mismatched pursuit status.
- No deal due to no pursuit.
- No deal due to no user consent.
- No deal due to user's objection to legitimate interest.

Figure 19: *Outcomes of Actions from a Publisher, a Vendor, and a User When a Publisher Transfers Data to a Vendor*

For Each Purpose		Vendor Option				
Publisher Option	User Decision	Only Consent	Only Leg. Int.	Default Leg. Int. but Consent Feasible	Default Consent but Leg. Int. Feasible	Do Not Pursue
Consent	Accept Consent	Deal upon Consent	No Deal due to Mismatched Legal Basis	Deal upon Consent	Deal upon Consent	No Deal due to Mismatched Pursuit
	Deny Consent	No Deal due to No User Consent	No Deal due to Mismatched Legal Basis	No Deal due to No User Consent	No Deal due to No User Consent	No Deal due to Mismatched Pursuit
Leg. Int.	Accept Leg. Int.	No Deal due to Mismatched Legal Basis	Deal upon Legitimate Interest	Deal upon Legitimate Interest	Deal upon Legitimate Interest	No Deal due to No Pursuit
	Deny Leg. Int.	No Deal due to User's Objection to Leg. Int.	No Deal due to Mismatched Legal Basis	No Deal due to User's Objection to Leg. Int.	No Deal due to User's Objection to Leg. Int.	No Deal due to Mismatched Pursuit
Do not Pursue	–	No Deal due to Mismatched Pursuit	No Deal due to Mismatched Pursuit	No Deal due to Mismatched Pursuit	No Deal due to Mismatched Pursuit	No Deal due to No Pursuit

Notes: Leg. Int. is the abbreviation for Legitimate Interest

In Figure 19, the cells in green represent a successful deal to transfer data from a publisher to a vendor for one of the purposes. The cells in red denote a failed deal to transfer data because the user does not give permission. The white cells represent no deal to transfer data because of a mismatch in the legal basis between what the publisher expects and what the vendor supports for the purpose. The cells in grey denote no deal to transfer data because either the publisher or the vendor, or both of them, do not pursue that purpose.

Overall, the TCF's standardized matching and checking procedure helps to ensure that a legal basis exists for a specified, explicit and legitimate purpose wherever data flows.

7.5.2 Facilitating Checking Permission for Data Transfer Between Vendors

In this section, we discuss the case where a vendor transfers data to another vendor. Checking the permission to process and transfer data is more straightforward for a vendor-to-vendor case than a publisher-to-vendor case. A vendor cannot use restrictions to adjust the legal basis for another vendor but only accepts whatever is disclosed in the GVL and stored in the TC string. Hence, a vendor can be in one of three states: (1) has user permission to process and transfer data (accept consent or accept legitimate interest), (2) does not have user permission to process and transfer data (deny consent or deny legitimate interest), or (3) does not pursue the purpose.

Figure 20: *Outcomes of States of Two Vendors When a Vendor Transfers Data to another Vendor*

For Each Purpose	Vendor 2		
Vendor 1	User Permission	No User Persmission	Do Not Pursue
User Permission	Deal upon Permission	No Deal due to No User Permission	No Deal due to Mismatched Pursuit
	No Deal due to No User Permission	No Deal due to No User Permission	No Deal due to Mismatched Pursuit
Do not Pursue	No Deal due to Mismatched Pursuit	No Deal due to Mismatched Pursuit	No Deal due to No Pursuit

Figure 20 summarizes the outcomes of data transfer between vendors. A vendor can only transfer personal data to another vendor if both vendors have the user's permissions, captured by the green cell. The cells in red depict a failed deal to transfer data because at least one of the vendors lacks user permission to process data for the purpose. The cells in grey represent no deal as at least one of the vendors does not pursue the purpose with user data.

7.6 Main Takeaways

The main takeaways from Section 7 are:

- A firm goes through three steps when getting permission for data processing, in order to supply a legal basis: (1) specifying purposes for data processing, (2) asking for and storing permission for the specified purposes, (3) checking permission for data transfer.

- The online advertising industry faces challenges for each of the three steps involved in getting permission for processing of personal data.

- The TCF is an industry initiative launched by IAB Europe, intending to tackle the challenges involved in getting permission for data processing by building up a standard for all participants to follow.

- TCF creates a uniform specification of purposes for data processing, shared by all participants, to prevent misunderstanding and help firms communicate conveniently with users and other firms.

- The TCF provides a Global Vendor List (GVL) to help vendors disclose their purposes, and publishers centralize and manage permission on behalf of their partner vendors.

- The TCF created the Transparency Consent string (TC string) to store, update and exchange a user's permission in a standardized way.

- The TCF provides no warranty for the GDPR compliance. Moreover, even with the help of the TCF, the procedure to handle and check permission remains complicated.

8

Empirical Examination of the Complexity of Getting Permission for Data Processing

8.1 Aim of the Empirical Study

Section 6 described the challenges for publishers and vendors in every step of getting permission for data processing towards supplying a legal basis in compliance with the GDPR. Although the TCF was designed to mitigate these challenges—by creating purpose specifications, tools, and rules—the procedures of getting permission are still complicated. Notably, firms' requirement to get permission for data processing imposes complexity not only on the firms themselves but also on users, who must handle cookie banners on numerous websites. Indeed, as elaborated in Section 6.2, only a few tools are available that support users in giving permission. In this section, we attempt to empirically quantify how complicated the process is regarding the amount of effort that firms and users have to invest in getting and providing permission, respectively. Such an assessment can point to directions that policymakers and actors in the online advertising market should focus on to facilitate the implementation of the GDPR, or to design new regulations.

We build our empirical analysis on the TCF, both because it is a prominent standard in the online advertising industry, and because it provides access to a great deal of publicly available information (e.g., GVL). For example, reliance on the TCF enables us to incorporate metrics such as the number of purposes each publisher and vendor pursues.

We divide our analysis into two parts. First, we focus on firms operating in the online advertising industry, evaluating the complexity of handling and checking permission—as reflected in the level of interconnectedness among firms. Second, we focus on users, examining the decision costs when giving and denying permission.

8.2 Data Collection and Description

To empirically analyze the process of getting permission for data processing, we sought to obtain data on (i) publishers that request user data, (ii) the vendors that each publisher collaborates with, and (iii) the purposes each vendor pursues. Accordingly, we combined two datasets, which we refer to as (1) a publisher–vendor (PV) dataset, and (2) a Global Vendor List (GVL) dataset.

The PV dataset is a list of publishers and of the vendors with whom they collaborate. Specifically, we focus on the 38 publishers among the Top 100 publishers in Germany (SimilarWeb web traffic ranking, December 2020) that use the TCF. To collect data about these publishers, we used a tool called "Consent Management Platform (CMP) Validator". The CMP Validator, which is a browser extension for Google Chrome, was developed by IAB Europe to check the validity of CMPs that register with the TCF. In practice, when one clicks on the extension from a publisher's webpage, a user interface pops up, as displayed in Figure 21. This user interface presents a list of the vendors with which the publisher collaborates, and it describes which legal bases each vendor uses to support its purposes on that publisher's webpage. It also outlines the TCF purposes and Special Features pursued by the publisher (on its own behalf and on behalf of its vendors) for each legal basis. We recorded all this information for each of our 38 publishers. Note that a publisher can also work with vendors who are not on the GVL, and these vendors do not appear on the list from the user interface.

Figure 21: *User Interface of the TCF CMP Validator*

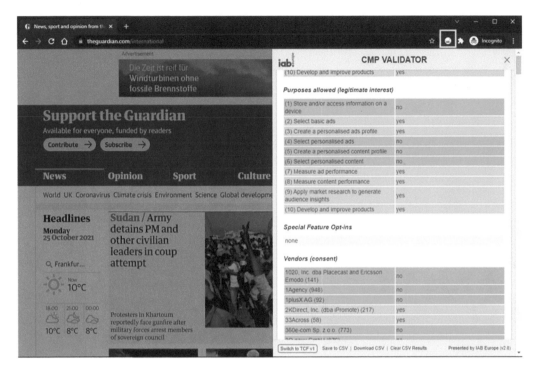

Notes: the top right yellow square highlights the icon of the CMP Validator extension

The CMP Validator does not specify the purposes pursued by each vendor. To obtain this information, we used the GVL dataset; see Sections 7.4.1.1 and 7.5.1 for information on what the GVL is and how it works to centralize vendors' permission requests. We obtained these data from the official website of the GVL (see www.iabeurope.eu/vendor-list; the website is updated every week, and IAB Europe also provides data via JSON files). The GVL dataset was based on the October 14, 2021 version of the GVL. This version of the GVL contained 803 vendors. Note that an increasing number of vendors have been getting on GVL since TCF 2.0 took effect. Figure 22 depicts the increase in the number of vendors on the GVL (Sep 2019 – Oct 2021). For each of the 803 vendors in the GVL dataset, we recorded the TCF purposes it pursues and the corresponding legal bases that support the TCF purposes.

Figure 22: *Development of Number of Vendors Participating in the TCF 2.0*

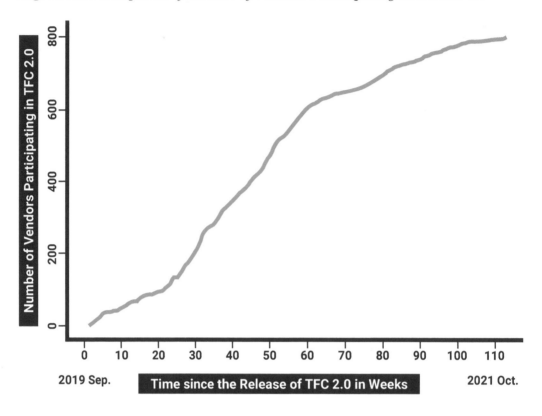

8.3 Examining the Complexity of Getting Permission for Actors in the Online Advertising Industry

8.3.1 Measurement of Complexity: Interconnectedness

In the first part of the analysis, we sought to measure the complexity that publishers face in getting permission for data processing (i.e., the amount of effort they must invest). To measure complexity, we evaluated the extent to which each of the 38 publishers in our PV dataset is interconnected with partner vendors. We operationalized interconnectedness as the number of vendors on the GVL that each publisher collaborates with, as indicated by the PV dataset. We focused on this measure because vendors rely on publishers to get permission on their behalf. Each publisher-vendor collaboration requires a separate process of collecting, storing, and checking user permission before sharing any personal data. Thus, the more vendors a publisher collaborates with, the more complexity it faces in getting permission. Note that there may be vendors that a publisher collaborates with that are not in the GVL hence not included in the PV dataset. Therefore, our measure might underestimate the complexity.

8.3.2 Description of Results

Figure 23 shows a histogram of the number of vendors on the GVL for each publisher in the PV dataset. On average, each publisher collaborates with 279.89 vendors. In other words, if a new user visits a publisher, then, on average, the publisher has to collect and store the user's permission for data processing on behalf of 279.89 vendors.

Figure 23: *Histogram of Number of Vendors on the GVL for each Publisher in the TCF*

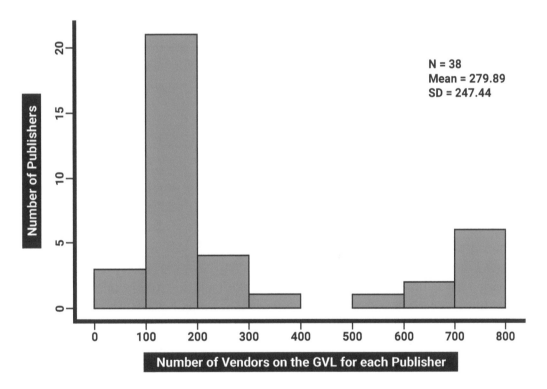

This finding suggests that publishers in the advertising industry have extensive interconnections with partner vendors, such that the process of getting permission for data processing is highly complex. One visit from a new user to a publisher triggers permission requests corresponding to hundreds of vendors, followed by storage of information and data transfers. Note that there are still cases where publishers display the full

GVL even though they do not collaborate with all registered vendors because they have not filtered out vendors with whom they are not actually working. Therefore, we might overestimate the complexity in these cases.

8.4 Examining the Complexity that Users Face in Making Decisions about Permission

8.4.1 Measurement of Complexity: Decision Costs

To measure the complexity users face as a result of firms' process of getting permission for data processing, we sought to calculate the decision costs of users when determining whether to give permission. The EU's guidelines (WP259) with regard to interpreting the GDPR's regulations on consent point out that granularity is one requirement for valid user permission; specifically, a user must have the chance to make different decisions on permission for each purpose of each vendor (European Data Protection Board 2020). However, regardless of whether a user gives permission or not, making decisions is costly in terms of effort and time, as the user is required, e.g., to read and process information.

To capture a user's decision costs, we used the number of decisions a user has to make on an average day when visiting an average number of websites, as well as the amount of time required to make these decisions.

We estimated the decision costs for users for the following three scenarios: In the first scenario, a user makes one decision for each purpose of each vendor (Case Heavy); this scenario captures a theoretical upper-bound estimate of the highest decision cost possible under the GDPR. In the second scenario, a user makes one decision for each vendor (Case Medium), regardless of the specific TCF purposes a vendor pursues; this scenario reflects the level of granularity that cookie banners typically offer in practice. In the third scenario, a user makes one decision for each TCF Stack, where a Stack is a pre-defined set of TCF purposes or Special Features (Case Light; see Section 7.3.3 for further details on Stacks); this scenario reflects a situation in which users make granular decisions while incurring the lowest possible decision costs. Consideration of these three scenarios enables us to obtain a comprehensive estimate of the decision costs that users with different preferences for decision granularity are likely to incur in practice. The three scenarios also enable us to capture the heterogeneity of publishers' purpose specifications and cookie banner designs. Table 16 shows examples of user decisions in the three scenarios.

Table 16: *Example of User Decisions in Case Heavy, Case Medium, and Case Light*

Label of Cases	User Makes Decisions on			Example of User Decisions Do you accept...	Description
	Each Vendor	Each Purpose	Each Stack		
Case Heavy	Yes	Yes	No	Vendor A using your data to: o Select personalized content o Select personalized ads	Different decisions on each purpose of each vendor
Case Medium	Yes	No	No	o Vendor Epsilon using your data to pursue all of the following: Select personalized content Select personalized ads	Different decisions on each legal basis of each vendor; Same decisions on all purposes of each vendor
Case Light	No	No	Yes	o All vendors to use your data to: Select personalized ads and content	Different decisions on each Stack; Same decisions on all vendors

Notes: a user makes one decision on each of the circles (o) in the examples

For each scenario, we used the PV dataset (which specifies publisher–vendor collaborations) together with the GVL dataset (which specifies the purposes that each vendor pursues) to estimate the number of decisions a user must make when visiting a given publisher for the first time.

Table 17 provides an example of how to calculate the number of user decisions for Case Heavy, Case Medium and Case Light.

Table 17: *Example for Calculating Number of User Decisions on Cookie Banner Settings for Scenarios Case Heavy, Case Medium, and Case Light*

	Number of Purposes (Legal Basis)	Special Features	Number of Decisions		
			Case Heavy	Case Medium	Case Light
Vendor 1	5 (5 Consent)	2	7	1	
Vendor 2	6 (2 Consent, 4 Leg. Int.)	0	6	2	
	......				
Vendor 155	10 (5 Consent, 5 Leg. Int.)	1	11	2	
Sum across Vendors			1,079	205	2

Notes: 1,079 is the sum of decisions across all vendors from Vendor 1 to Vendor 155.

Leg. Int. is the abbreviation for legitimate interest.

Reading example: The value of the cell "Vendor 1, case heavy" is 7 because the user has to make 1 decision for each of the 5 Purposes and the 2 Special Features. The value of the cell "Vendor 2 and case medium" is 2 because the user has to make 1 decision for all Purposes and Special Features based on Consent and 1 decision for all Purposes based on legitimate interest.

On the basis of our PV dataset, we determine that Fandom.com collaborates with 155 vendors. For each of these vendors, we use the GVL dataset to quantify the number of user decisions the vendor requires—namely, the number of TCF purposes and Special Features that the vendor pursues. (Recall that, as summarized in Figure 15, users can only make decisions with regard to TCF purposes (give consent or object to legitimate interest) and Special Features (give consent).) In the Fandom.com example, Vendor 1 pursues five out of the ten possible TCF purposes and uses both Special Features. Hence, the total number of decisions a user makes for Vendor 1 is 7. We repeat this calculation for the remaining vendors (obtaining 6 decisions for Vendor 2, 11 decisions for Vendor 155, etc.). Summing up the number of decisions for the 155 vendors, we obtain a total of 1,079 decisions. We carry out this calculation for each publisher. In Case Heavy, we only focus on the decisions a user makes for the vendors and neglect the decisions for the publisher (the decision for Fandom.com itself in the example).

In Case Medium, a user makes one decision for each legal basis each vendor uses. It often results in two decisions: one for all purposes and Special Features requiring consent and one for all purposes that use legitimate interest. This scenario corresponds to most cookie banners, which enable users to give consent on a vendor level. In the example of Table 17, if a user gives consent to Vendor 1, then, in a single decision, the user provides consent for the vendor's five TCF purposes and two Special Features. For Vendor 2, the user must make two vendor-level decisions rather than one, because Vendor 2 pursues two different legal bases, and the user makes separate decisions for each legal basis (e.g., the user might make a decision to permit both purposes supported by consent, and a decision to object to all four purposes supported by legitimate interest). The final result is the sum of decisions across all vendors.

Figure 24: *Example of a Publisher Using Stacks to Get User's Permission (here: theguardian.com)*

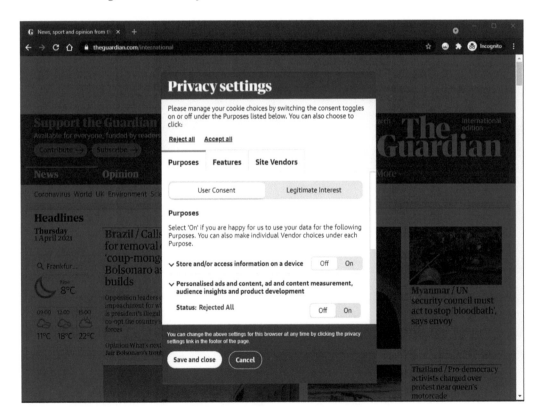

In Case Light, we assume that a user is presented with Stacks (see details in Section 7.3.3). Figure 24 shows an example of a cookie banner from TheGuardian.com, which contains two Stacks. In this example, a user makes two decisions, one for each Stack.

According to a manual check of the Top 100 publishers in Germany using Stacks, most publishers use two Stacks (e.g., WEB.DE, GMX.net). Therefore, we assume that, in Case Light, a user makes two decisions for each publisher.

8.4.2 Description of Results

8.4.2.1 Number of User Decisions

We calculated the number of user decisions for each publisher and for all three cases by summing up the number of decisions across all vendors with whom the publisher collaborates. The result for Case heavy is that a user needs to make 1,896.61 decisions on average for a publisher. Figure 25 displays how the number of decisions varies for each publisher.

Figure 25: *Histogram of Number of User Decisions on Cookie Banner for each Publisher in Scenario Case Heavy*

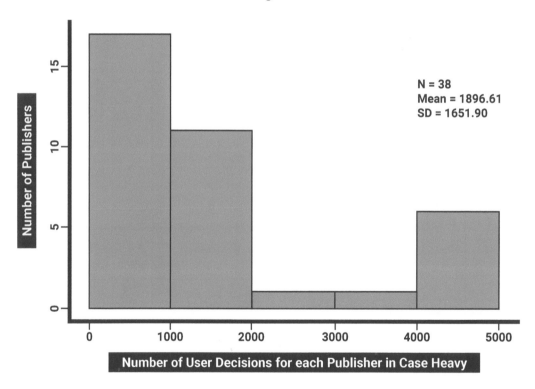

Figure 26 illustrates the results for Case Medium. In this scenario, an average user makes 364.89 decisions for each publisher. Although the number of decisions, in this case, is substantially lower than those in Case Heavy (1,896.61 decisions), making hundreds of decisions is hardly feasible. We will further elaborate on this point by estimating the time spent making decisions in Section 8.4.2.2.

Figure 26: *Histogram of Number of User Decisions on Cookie Banner for each Publisher in Scenario Case Medium*

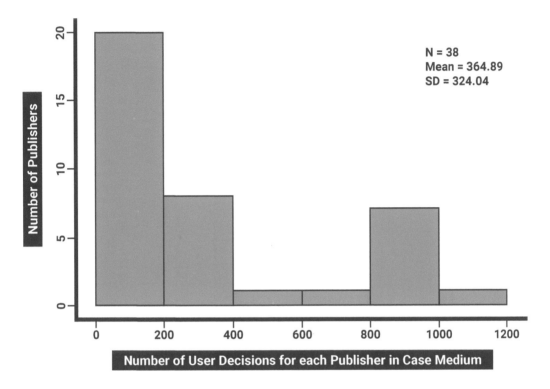

For Case Light, as discussed in the previous subsection, we assume that an average user makes two decisions for each publisher.

8.4.2.2 Time Spent on Making Decisions

To provide a more intuitive illustration of user decision costs, we transform the average number of user decisions into time spent making decisions. To carry out this transformation, we make several assumptions. First, we assume that it takes a user one second to read the respective information on the cookie banner and to make one decision. We further assume that it takes seven seconds to load a cookie banner, including the different layers, for each website. These assumptions for decision time and loading time are based on simulations in which we visited several publishers, made decisions, and recorded the amount of time spent.

We also assume that an average user spends four minutes reading the content of one website. The rationale for this assumption is presented in Table 18, which shows calculations capturing the heterogeneity of content-reading time across devices, namely mobile, desktop and tablet. The first row of Table 18 contains the average amount of time (in seconds) spent on a single website on each device; these values are based on a report by the digital consultancy firm Perficient (Enge 2021). The second row of Table 18 transforms these values into minutes. We observe that, on average, a reader spends four minutes reading content on a single website on a single device.

Table 18: *Calculation of Content Reading Time and the Number of Daily Visited Websites*

Variables for Calculation	Calculation	Results				
		Mobile	**Desktop**	**Tablet**	**Overall**	**Average**
Average time on each website via this device (sec)	(1)	159.21	323.47	236.85	NA	239.84
Average time on each website via this device (min)	$(2) = \dfrac{(1)}{60}$	2.65	5.39	3.95	NA	**4.00**
Share of time spent on this device among all types of devices	(3)	61%	36%	3%	100%	
Daily time spent on visiting websites via this device (min)	$(4) = \dfrac{25}{61\%} \cdot (3)$	25	14.75	1.23	40.98	
Number of websites visited on this device	$(5) = \dfrac{(4)}{(2)}$	9.42	2.74	0.31	**12.47**	

Notes: Numbers in black are inputs, numbers in blue are outputs from the calculation. The second column either labels an input or displays the equation of how an output is calculated and labels the output.

We further propose that the average user visits 12.47 websites each day. The rationale for this assumption is also elaborated in Table 18. Specifically, the third row of the table contains the share of time that a user spends browsing content on a given device, relative to all time spent browsing content online (Enge 2021). Combining these values with Wurmser (2021) finding that the average user spends 25 minutes per day visiting websites on mobile devices, we calculate the average daily time spent on other devices according to their respective shares. The fourth row of Table 18 shows the results. Dividing the average daily time spent on all websites by the average daily time spent on each website gives the number of websites visited on each device. The bottom row of Table 18 displays the results, with 12.47 being the average number of websites visited each day across devices.

Finally, we assume that on 20% of the websites that a user visits, a new cookie banner pops up to which the user must respond. The assumption is supported by a calculation in which we divide the number of unique visitors of a typical publisher, T-Online.de, in Jan 2021 (Statista) by the number of visitors (SimilarWeb).

Table 19 summarizes the various assumptions.

Table 19: *Summary of Assumptions for Decision Time Calculation*

Variables for Decision Time Calculation	Assumptions
Time spent making each decision	1 second
Time spent loading each cookie banner	7 seconds
Time spent reading the content of each website	4 minutes
Number of websites visited each day	12.47
Share of websites requiring consent decisions	20%

On the basis of these assumptions, we calculate the amount of time that a user spends per day making decisions. Table 20 provides an illustration of this calculation for Case Light. Recall that in Case Light a user makes two decisions on each website. Therefore, it takes 9 seconds for the user to make decisions on one website (7 seconds loading time plus 1 second for each decision), which equals 0.15 minutes. On average, a user visits 2.49 websites per day that require consent decisions. Hence, in Case Light, a user spends 0.37 minutes per day making decisions on cookie banners. An average user spends 49.85 minutes reading the content of websites each day and spends 50.22 minutes overall visiting websites. The share of browsing time spent on making decisions is 0.74%. The number of additional websites that could have been visited if not making decisions is 0.09.

Table 20: *Calculation of User Decision Time on Cookie Banner in Scenario Case Light*

Variables for Calculation	Calculation	Results	
		In Minutes	In Seconds
Time spent reading the content of each website	(1)	4	240
Number of websites visited each day	(2)	12.47	
Time spent reading the content of all websites visited each day	$(3) = (1) \cdot (2)$	49.85	2,991
Share of websites requiring consent decisions	(4)	20%	
Number of websites requiring consent decision	$(5) = (2) \cdot (4)$	2.49	
Number of decisions on each website	(6)	2	
Time spent making each decision	(7)	0.02	1
Time spent loading each cookie banner	(8)	0.12	7
Time spent making decisions on each website	$(9) = (6) \cdot (7) + (8)$	0.15	9
Time spent making decisions on all websites visited each day	$(10) = (5) \cdot (9)$	0.37	22
Time spent making decisions and reading content on all websites visited each day	$(11) = (3) + (10)$	50.22	3,013
Share of browsing time spent on making decisions	$(12) = \dfrac{(10)}{(11)}$	0.74%	
Number of additional websites that could have been visited if not making decisions	$(13) = \dfrac{(10)}{(1)}$	0.09	

Notes: The second column either labels an input or displays the equation of how the output is calculated.

Table 21 summarizes the results for each of the three scenarios. Under Case Heavy, an average user spends 79.13 minutes per day (approx. 1.5 hours), making the most granular decisions possible, covering 61% of the user's overall browsing time. Had the user not spent this time making decisions, she could have visited 19.79 more publisher websites. The decision cost for this scenario is so high that it hampers a user's browsing experience by taking up 61% of the entire browsing time. In practice, this case is hardly feasible.

Table 21: *Summary of User Decision Cost Estimation under Different Scenarios*

Measurement of Decision Cost	Case Heavy	Case Medium	Case Light
Number of user decisions	1,896.61	364.89	2.00
Time spent making decisions for publisher websites each day (min)	79.13	15.46	0.37
Share of browsing time spent on making decisions	61%	24%	0.74%
Number of publisher websites that could have been loaded if not making decisions	19.79	3.87	0.09

In Case Medium, the average user spends 15.46 minutes per day making decisions on permissions, 24% of the overall browsing time. Had she not spent this time making decisions, the user could have visited 3.87 more publisher websites. For many users, 15.46 minutes per day might be too costly to spend.

In Case Light, as noted above, the average user spends 0.37 minutes per day making decisions, covering 0.74% of the total browsing time. It seems that the use of Stacks could reduce users' decision time to a feasible level while maintaining some granularity.

8.5 Main Takeaways

The main takeaways from Section 8 are:

- The average publisher collaborates with 279.89 vendors. This high interconnectedness of the online advertising industry suggests that publishers and vendors face high complexity when getting permission.

- On average, each user visits 2.49 new publishers per day. If a user were to make all possible decisions regarding the provision of permission for data processing (Case Heavy), she would spend 31.65 minutes per publisher, resulting in a decision time of 79.13 minutes per day.

- Given the high decision time associated with making all possible decisions, it seems that both publishers and users can benefit from the use of Stacks, which facilitates the user's decisions by letting the user address many vendors and purposes simultaneously (Case Light). The use of Stacks shortens the decision time to 0.37 minutes per day.

9

Outlook on Further Developments

The GDPR has inspired firms to change their operations in other ways beyond those discussed in previous sections. Some of these activities aim to decrease personal data processing (Section 9.1), whereas others aim to increase it (Section 9.2).

9.1 Activities that Aim to Decrease the Processing of Personal Data

Firms take several avenues to decrease the processing of personal data, some building upon privacy laws and some going beyond existing regulations. These activities might result from different motivations. On the one hand, a firm might decrease personal data processing to fulfill user preferences for higher consumer privacy. On the other hand, the firm might be motivated by the competitive effect and aims to strengthen its market position relative to its competitors by being more privacy-focused.

One action that firms have taken and are taking is changing the default settings they offer users in privacy decisions. An increasing number of web browsers and devices did so. So, instead of merely offering the option to block tracking if a user prefers this configuration, they have started to block tracking technologies such as third-party cookies by default. For example, Safari started to block certain third-party cookies in 2017 and to completely block tracking in 2020, and Firefox has blocked third-party cookies since 2019. Chrome has also announced that it will begin to block third-party cookies from 2023 on. Additionally, device manufacturers have started to adjust the default settings for mobile phones. For example, the firm Volla created a smartphone that, by default, blocks any tracking of the user and builds upon an operating system independent of Google and its operating system, Android, or other players.

Apple introduced the App Tracking Transparency framework (ATT) with the 14.5 iOS update in April 2021. Essentially, ATT requires app developers to ask users for consent if they want to track consumers. The app developers request consent via a so-called "ATT prompt", similar to cookie banners on websites, and need to outline the purpose of tracking. The developer can decide when to ask the user for consent but cannot access the user's identifier before receiving the user's consent.

However, one significant difference between the GDPR and Apple's privacy activities is the regional scope. While the GDPR is limited to EU firms and all other firms that cater to EU users, Apple's privacy activities apply globally to all Apple users. In certain parts of the world, Apple's privacy activities, particularly the consent requirement, are stricter than local privacy laws, such as in California, where the local privacy law (CCPA) only requires an opt-out possibility. Thus, private firms such as Apple implicitly introduce privacy regulations.

Google's privacy sandbox aims at decreasing the processing of personal data while maintaining the value of the information derived from users' browsing behavior. The privacy sandbox introduced several approaches, including the (i) "Federated Learning of Cohorts" (FLoC) for targeting specific groups of users, and (ii) "Two uncorrelated requests, then locally executed decisions on victory (and an e)" (Turtledove) specifically for retargeting. Both approaches aim to keep the tracking, profiling, and targeting of a user in the user's browser. Therefore, fewer user data move outside the browser towards third parties, instead of remaining close to the user, namely in the user's browser. Moreover, these approaches likely increase the reach of Google ads remarkably because Google might show ads to all Chrome users on every website.

FLoC represents an approach in which Google classifies Chrome users into large groups according to their past browsing behavior. Advertisers then receive information about these groups and no longer about individual users. Consequently, they can only target groups of individuals and not individuals. However, privacy advocates have raised concerns that this approach might actually increase user tracking because Google could group users based on their entire browsing behavior. In addition, some publishers have already announced intentions to block FLoC (e.g., WordPress, Amazon), partly because Google could use its browser to track users on websites that are unrelated to its business. Thus, Google might not continue to pursue FLoC but propose alternatives instead.

Turtledove represents a new and more privacy-compliant approach in which advertisers can retarget users but do not get access to personal data. This approach uses two kinds of information: (i) about advertisers stored in the user's browser (e.g., a user visited the advertiser's online store some time ago) and (ii) about the website a user is currently visiting. Then, the browser conducts an auction and requests that advertisers place two bids: one for the first kind of information (i) and one for the second kind (ii). Those two requests are independent of each other from the advertisers' perspective. The advertiser with the highest bid across both requests wins the auction. The most recent version of Turtledove is "First Locally-Executed Decision over Groups Experiment" (FLEDGE), which includes industry suggestions, such as incorporating a trusted server to store information about a campaign's bids and budgets.

Microsoft proposes with "Private and Anonymized Requests for Ads that Keep Efficacy and Enhance Transparency" (PARAKEET) an alternative to Google's privacy sandbox. It also uses a trusted server but builds upon differential privacy to anonymize personal data. More specifically, the proposal aims to decrease the accuracy of users' personal data to protect their privacy without decreasing the data's value severely.

The activities mentioned above aim to decrease the processing of personal data. These activities likely reduce the number of tracked users and the amount of data available to firms in the online advertising industry. As a result, advertisers' targeting ability might diminish, leading ad prices to decrease, along with publishers' revenue.

9.2 Activities that Aim to Increase the Processing of Personal Data

The limitations imposed by the GDPR have also motivated firms to identify means of increasing the processing of personal data, using monetary and non-monetary incentives. Most importantly, publishers have started to implement so-called "cookie paywalls."

Essentially, cookie paywalls allow users access to the publisher's content either if (i) the user provides permission for their personal data to be processed for online advertising purposes (which often includes profiling and targeting), or if (ii) the user pays a subscription fee to the publisher. Often, this subscription fee to avoid tracking also includes an advertising-free subscription. In Germany and Austria, some publishers (e.g., Spiegel, Zeit, Standard) refer to cookie paywalls as the "PUR" (i.e., "purity model", see Section 5.2.2.2). In addition to individual publisher solutions to implement such a "PUR", there also exist solutions that aim at bundling publishers so that the user pays a subscription fee for a set of publishers together (e.g., contentpass from Germany).

Cookie paywalls introduce a new barrier to accessing content free of (monetary) charge and constitute a trade-off between the user being tracked, profiled and targeted, or paying for the publisher's content. This approach might lead to unequal treatment of users visiting a publisher's website. A user with lower income may be more likely to wish to avoid paying money for the publisher's content and thus to either pay with data or move to a different publisher, which may offer content of lower quality.

Another initiative that firms have adopted is providing the user with a monetary incentive to allow user tracking. For example, the firm Gener8 implemented a browser that offers users a choice between two options. The first option for users is to block tracking while also indicating their preferences for certain topics (on an optional basis); this option enables users to enjoy a tracking-free experience while still providing adequate targeting opportunities for advertisers. The second option for users is to allow tracking but to earn points for allowing it. Users can then redeem these points to get discounts, free trials and even free products from cooperating firms.

Such an initiative is beneficial for users and firms alike: Users can choose their preferred way of browsing—tracking-free or with tracking—and get compensated for allowing tracking if they choose to do so. Furthermore, even if users decide to block tracking, advertisers are still able to target users, based on their explicitly reported preferences.

Another initiative for increasing user tracking is netID, developed by the European netID Foundation, a foundation created by an alliance of publishers. Currently, more than 100 publishers implement netID, aiming to decrease the number of user accounts and login credentials per user and replace them with one account. The basic premise of netID is that it provides a user with a single account that can be used to access different publishers, and the user manages all permission decisions within that netID account. This centralization is likely to reduce the decision costs that users face when providing and managing permission for data processing. Therefore, in effect, netID provides non-monetary incentives to use netID.

The activities mentioned above aim to increase the processing of personal data. Therefore, they likely enable advertisers to target advertisements better, increasing the respective ad prices, potentially enabling publishers to gain more revenue from ad sales and to improve the quality of their content.

9.3 Outlook on Further Regulatory Activities

The introduction of the GDPR sparked several additional regulatory initiatives that warrant discussion, including the following: (i) the Digital Services Act, (ii) the Digital Markets Act, (iii) the ePrivacy Regulation, and (iv) the Tracking-Free Ads Coalition. Moreover, the introduction of the GDPR as a European standard might lead to (v) deviations in terms of its interpretation and enforcement.

9.3.1 Digital Services Act

The Digital Services Act (DSA) is a legislative proposal concerning illegal content, transparent advertising, and disinformation. It was proposed on Dec 15, 2020, by the European Commission to update the e-Commerce Directive 2000. The new obligation concerning the online advertising industry is that a firm must disclose to users, in real-time, three kinds of information: (1) that they are seeing an advertisement, (2) who is providing this ad, and (3) the main parameters applied to determine why this ad targets the user. Firms that do not comply with the DSA risk a fine of up to 6% on their global annual turnover.

The DSA may impact the online advertising industry in two ways. First, the competitive advantage brought by algorithms for ad targeting is likely to decrease. Algorithms play a key role in determining how well an ad targets the desired user, hence ad effectiveness. Since the new obligation requires the main parameters for ad targeting to be made publicly available, firms will learn more about their competitors' algorithms. Consequently, a firm might need to either improve its algorithms more rapidly than its competitors to maintain a competitive advantage or identify other ways to improve ad effectiveness.

Second, firms are likely to find it challenging to determine how to display the required three kinds of information. Designing and running cookie banners has posed challenges to the online advertising industry already (Section 7.1.1). According to the new regulation, whenever a user sees an ad, a firm will be required to display a great deal of information about the targeted ad. Simply piling the information on top of the ad might make the appearance messy, triggering annoyance toward the ads. IAB Europe aims to support the industry in addressing these concerns by developing new approaches and technical standards to provide users with valid messages regarding the targeted ads they see.

Overall, as a result of the DSA, firms in the online advertising industry will likely have to pay higher costs to maintain the current level of ad effectiveness, and will have to make additional investments in order to display required information without inducing user annoyance. As a result, profits in the online advertising industry might decrease.

9.3.2 Digital Markets Act

The Digital Markets Act (DMA) is a proposal focusing on actors in the online advertising industry with considerable market power, regarded as "gatekeepers" in the industry. A gatekeeper significantly impacts the internal market, acting as an important gateway for firms using the gatekeeper's services to reach their users (European Commission 2021). The DMA was proposed on Dec 15, 2020, by the European Commission. The regulation aims to ensure an adequate level of competition in European digital markets. The DMA creates criteria for recognizing a firm as a gatekeeper and sets rules for these firms. The gatekeepers come from many sectors, including the online advertising industry. Gatekeeper firms that are not compliant with the DMA risk a fine of up to 10% on their annual turnover.

Once in effect, the DMA will identify gatekeepers in the online advertising industry with clearly defined conditions: (1) significant impact on the internal market and active in multiple EU countries (e.g., annual turnover exceeding 6.5€ billion in the last three financial years), (2) strong intermediation position (e.g., has over 10,000 yearly active business partners in the EU), (3) stable and durable market position. The identified gatekeepers must comply with the prohibitions and obligations of the DMA.

The obligations include allowing any business partner (e.g., a small vendor) to access data that the gatekeeper (e.g., a large publisher) has collected with regard to users' interactions with the partner. This access means, for example, that a gatekeeper like Facebook can no longer keep all user data to itself; a small- or medium-sized firm that posts ads on Facebook must be provided with access to the data that Facebook has collected regarding users' interactions with those ads, thereby enabling the smaller firm to carry out its own verification and analysis of ad performance. The obligations imposed by the DMA also prohibit the gatekeeper from discriminating in favor of its own services. For example, when working with publishers, a gatekeeper like Google (as a vendor) cannot treat its own Ad Technology Provider controls more favorably than other third-party frameworks that assist firms in asking for and managing user permission, such as TCF 2.0. Jürgensmeier and Skiera (2022) suggest an approach to measure the fair treatment of participants on an online platform.

The DSA will make part of a gatekeeper's user data available for small and medium-sized firms. The small and medium-sized firms can draw on these data to improve the performance of online advertising via profiling and targeting, thereby potentially increasing their profits. In turn, the competitive advantage of the gatekeeper, which is often based on its exclusive access to user data, might decrease, thereby decreasing the gatekeeper's profit.

9.3.3 ePrivacy Regulation

The ePrivacy Regulation (ePR) regulates various privacy-related topics, mainly concerning electronic communications within the European Union. It was initially proposed in 2017 by the European Commission to repeal the Privacy and Electronic Communications Directive 2002 (the so-called ePrivacy Directive (ePD)) and to complement the GDPR. Initially, the ePrivacy Regulation was supposed to go into effect with the GDPR on May 25, 2018, but it still has not been adopted.

The ePrivacy Regulation proposes that users give their consent on a device level rather than on a website level, as is the current practice under the GDPR. For every internet browser on the user's desktop, smartphone, or tablet, a user would have to permit or restrict tracking and the usage of the user's data by websites. Such device-level consent would considerably reduce the number of decisions per user, reduce the decision cost per user, and improve the user's online browsing experience.

In addition to gathering a user's consent at the device level, the ePrivacy Regulation also suggests limiting the time that a user's consent is valid. Thus, instead of websites obtaining a user's consent "forever," it would be limited to a pre-specified period, e.g., 6 or 12 months.

Potentially moving consent to the device (browser) level could reduce the importance of CMPs for publishers if the devices (via browsers) implement their functionality. A downside of moving a user's consent decision to the device–browser level instead of deciding on every website is that a user does not have any information on the specific websites and apps asking for the user's permission. Therefore, such a practice is likely to result in most users refusing to consent to data sharing—thereby removing large amounts of data from the online advertising industry. For advertisers, as discussed above, less access to data implies fewer opportunities to target users, which, in turn, decreases ad prices and ultimately reduces publishers' ad revenue. IAB Europe (2021a) predicts that enforcement of the ePrivacy Regulation would reduce half of the revenues of the online advertising industry in the EU.

9.3.4 Tracking-Free Ads Coalition

The Tracking-Free Ads Coalition is a coalition of members of the European Parliament, civil society organizations, and firms from across the EU. It aims at ending tracking, profiling, and targeting of users by the online advertising industry. The coalition thinks that online advertising can finance free content on the Internet even without behavioral targeting that relies on tracking and profiling users. The coalition wants to achieve its aims through EU legislation and concrete action to support and complement existing legal frameworks such as the GDPR.

If the Tracking-Free Ads Coalition successfully stopped user tracking entirely, the online advertising industry could no longer use behavioral targeting. A benefit of such a situation for both the user and the industry would be that user consent for user tracking and subsequent profiling and targeting would become unnecessary. In such a case, the user's decision costs and firms' costs for getting and storing permission would be reduced to zero, as firms would no longer process personal data for online behavioral advertising.

Instead, advertisers would increasingly have to use other forms of online advertising that do not rely on user tracking, such as contextual advertising, with lower targeting efficiency than behavioral targeting. In addition, it is also not clear if some of the current forms of contextual targeting could prevail, given some of them also rely on the processing of personal data. For example, tracking the success of contextual ad campaigns on an individual user level processes personal data.

9.3.5 Deviations of the GDPR's Interpretation and Enforcement

A key potential benefit of the GDPR, as well as of other European privacy initiatives, is the notion of a single "European standard"—in which many firms, spanning many countries, become subject to similar requirements. Such standardization provides many advantages, particularly for firms whose economic activities encompass multiple European countries. However, these advantages diminish if member states of the European Union deviate from the "European standard". Such deviations can occur if countries interpret and enforce the "European standard" differently or even do not enforce the GDPR at all (e.g., Lukic, Miller, and Skiera 2022). Even worse, countries consist of different regions or states, and deviations might occur within these states. For example, in Germany, the Data Protection Authority of the state of Hamburg, as the Austrian DPA, interprets the cookie paywall implemented by publishers in Hamburg as being GDPR-compliant. It is doubtful that the Data Protection Authorities of other states (e.g., Baden-Wuerttemberg) would have drawn the same conclusion. Moreover, some privacy advocates complain about unsolved complaints about privacy abuses. For example, they argue that Ireland (Germany) left 192 of 196 (124 out of 176) complaints unsolved in 2020, indicating the different enforcement across countries (Owen 2021).

Unfortunately, such deviations contradict the vision of having one "European standard" and might ultimately also hurt European users.

Regional differences in interpretation and enforcement notwithstanding, the GDPR is far-reaching with its global scope, in saying that it applies to all European users, no matter where the base location of the firm is. Other upcoming privacy laws might take a similar approach—which might raise new questions in situations that require compliance with multiple laws that contradict each other. For example, each privacy law might require that a firm store the data in its country and nowhere else, or for a specific duration.

9.4 Outlook on Further Activities of Consumer Protection Agencies

The introduction of the GDPR also triggered new initiatives by consumer protection agencies. We describe two of them in more detail: None of Your Business (Section 9.4.1) and the Irish Council for Civil Liberties (Section 9.4.2).

9.4.1 None of Your Business (NOYB)

The European Center for Digital Rights, known as "none of your business" (NOYB), is a non-profit organization established in 2017, led by Austrian lawyer and privacy activist Max Schrems. With a focus on privacy issues in the private sector, NOYB aims to support the enforcement of the GDPR, the ePrivacy Regulation, and privacy regulations in general. The primary action of NOYB is filing complaints against firms to Data Protection Authorities and bringing cases to courts. The complaints cover various topics, including data transfer to non-EU areas, online and mobile tracking, and data breaches. For example, NOYB filed several complaints against large news websites in Germany and Austria against the PUR model (see Section 5.2.2.2). NOYB doubts that the user's consent is still freely given in such a cookie paywall business model. Moreover, NOYB launches media initiatives to disseminate knowledge of data privacy. For example, the website GDPRhub wiki contains databases that summarize Data Protection Authorities' and courts' decisions, commentaries, and profiles. Meanwhile, NOYB conducts research and develops tools that support privacy (e.g., the "advanced data protection control" (ADPC) browser extension, see Section 6.2.2).

On May 31, 2021, NOYB sent over 500 draft complaints to publishers with unlawful cookie banners. A publisher who has received a draft complaint can go to NOYB's WeComply! Platform to review the case of violation, download a guide on remedying the situation, and report full compliance. A draft complaint will turn into a formal one if the cookie banner of the publisher under investigation has not turned lawful within one month.

NOYB's criteria for a lawful cookie banner are strict, and other authorities may not agree with them (IAB Europe 2021b). Such disagreement may be a consequence of the fact that consumer protection agencies have largely been absent from consultations within the online advertising industry. More broadly, NOYB's campaign may serve as a signal to the online advertising industry that grey areas regarding interpretations of the GDPR are likely to shrink after the court judgments on the large wave of complaints. These complaints may also influence firms' choices with regard to the locations of their headquarters: Since complaints always go to local Data Protection Authorities where the headquarters of firms are situated, firms may strategically choose to locate their head-quarters in places where Data Protection Authorities interpret regulations more loosely.

The strict rules for cookie banners set by NOYB are likely to prevent circumstances in which users are lured into accepting data processing. Therefore, the activities of NOYB may ultimately limit the number of users that can be tracked, thereby diminishing the amount of data available for tracking, profiling, and targeting. Consequently, ad prices may decrease, reducing publishers' revenues.

9.4.2 Irish Council for Civil Liberties

In early 2018, Dr. Johnny Ryan contacted Data Protection Authorities in Ireland and the UK to "blow the whistle" about a massive data breach within the online advertising in-dustry's real-time bidding (RTB) system. One of the main criticisms is that any data that the publisher reveals in RTB can spread to many other actors. Johnny Ryan outlines that it is technically feasible to share a wide range of personal data along the chain outlined in Figure 6. He presented evidence showing that real-time bidding data had allegedly been used to influence a Polish election, to profile Irish people who secretly have HIV, and to track homeless people's movements in San Francisco. Such sharing raises pri-vacy concerns, in particular, as the user most often did not provide consent for sharing personal data. It is, however, less apparent if and to what extent sharing actually occurs (Ada, Abou Nabout, and McDonnell Feit 2022).

In November 2021, the Belgian Data Protection Authority (APD) announced that it is close to finalizing a draft ruling on its investigation of the RTB ecosystem and specifically IAB Europe's role within the Transparency and Consent Framework (TCF). The draft ruling will identify infringements of the GDPR by IAB Europe. Still, it will also find that those infringements should be capable of being remedied within six months following the issuing of the final ruling, in a process that would involve the APD overseeing the execution of an agreed action plan by IAB Europe.

10

Summary and Conclusions

10.1 Summary

As regulators worldwide are introducing new laws to protect users' privacy, this book has sought to fill crucial gaps in our understanding of how these laws affect the online advertising industry—where publishers and advertisers rely on user data to sustain many aspects of their operations. We focused our discussion on one of the first and most all-encompassing privacy laws, the European General Data Protection Regulation (GDPR), whose scope extends to any firm that is based in the EU or that serves EU or non-EU citizens.

Our major insights include the following:

- The operations of the online advertising industry are grounded in agreements—some implicit—between three main actors: the publisher, the user, and the advertiser. The publisher provides the user with content—in many cases free of (monetary) charge—in exchange for the opportunity to track and profile the user (i.e., the user's personal data). The publisher gains revenue by providing information on the user to advertisers, which use it for targeting, thereby improving ad performance.

- An increase in privacy protection endangers the implicit agreements between the parties because it reduces advertisers' ability to behaviorally target users, thereby reducing their willingness to pay to serve ads on publishers' websites. The resulting loss in revenue could force publishers to seek cost-saving measures—e.g., reducing the quality or quantity of their content—or to activate other revenue sources, e.g., via paywalls for their content. These measures may diminish the user's experience.

- The GDPR was one of the first strict privacy laws to be introduced; others have since emerged and continue to emerge worldwide. Thus, the GDPR "paved the way" for other countries to follow. Notably, and perhaps most concerningly for firms, the GDPR enables non-compliant firms to be penalized with very high fines (the greater of up to 4% of a firm's global annual turnover or €20 million). These penalties substantially exceed those imposed by other privacy laws, except those of China's privacy law (PIPL).

- The GDPR is remarkable because it applies not only to the data processing activities of European firms but also to those of any firm worldwide that deals with European users.

- The GDPR introduced new obligations—and thus new costs—for firms operating in the advertising industry. Notably, firms' compliance with these obligations entails costs for the user as well.

- One of the key obligations introduced by the GDPR is the need for firms to supply a legal basis in order to implement tracking technologies for personal data processing, including personal data collection. The relevant legal bases for online advertising are users' explicit consent or legitimate interest. These two legal bases differ in that users' consent represents an opt-in approach, whereas legitimate interest is an opt-out approach. Courts tend to favor users' consent over legitimate interest.

- Obtaining user permission for personal data processing is technically challenging, and consent management platforms (CMPs) have emerged as a new actor in the online advertising industry to assist firms in coping with the challenges they face.

- Obtaining user permission for personal data processing is particularly challenging for firms that do not serve as publishers (e.g., firms identified as "vendors" in the TCF) and thus do not have direct contact with users. These firms need to rely on a publisher to obtain user permission on their behalf.

- Firms, especially vendors, have an obligation to delete the collected personal data when users withdraw consent or want to delete their personal data. So far, this obligation has always been neglected to regulate.

- The GDPR defines two categories of firms with regard to their obligations in processing personal data: data controllers and data processors. Data controllers (often publishers) have more obligations than do data processors (often vendors). In particular, data controllers are responsible for the legal compliance of all cooperating data processors. Thus, data controllers need to carefully select the data processors with whom they collaborate.

- Firms in the online advertising industry are highly interconnected, with each publisher collaborating on average with 278 vendors. This interconnectivity makes coordination among actors challenging and requires sophisticated technologies.

- Processing personal data becomes easier if data controllers and data processors use a "common language" to define the purposes for which they seek permission for personal data processing, as well as standardized procedures for the transfer of information. The TCF is a framework that aims to provide such standards, thereby facilitating the free flow of personal data.

- The vision of the GDPR to put users in control of their personal data also requires users to make decisions regarding the permissions they provide. If users wanted to make an explicit decision for each request to process personal data, it would take up 61% of their time visiting websites.

- Firms have various tools to facilitate compliance with the GDPR, including CMPs and the TCF. Yet, hardly any tools support users' decision processes and permission management costs.

10.2 Conclusions

There is virtually no doubt that the GDPR represents a milestone in enabling users to achieve higher control over their (relatively broadly defined) personal data. However, the introduction of the GDPR has also stimulated a wide range of discussions among data protection authorities, firms, industry initiatives and consumer advocates on the implications of complying with the GDPR and how best to achieve such compliance—as well as more fundamental questions regarding what the true value of user privacy is, and how best to provide users with the optimal level of privacy.

Indeed, as always, there is no free lunch, and protection of user privacy comes at a cost to firms in the advertising industry, and even to users and to society at large. In this book, we have attempted to provide a nuanced yet comprehensive understanding of some of these costs. Academic studies have begun to provide empirical evidence of the toll that the GDPR may be taking: For example, one study suggests that the GDPR has reduced firms' innovation activities (Janssen et al. 2021), and others show that less tracking leads to lower advertising revenue for publishers (Johnson, Shriver, and Du 2020, Laub, Miller, and Skiera 2022). The resulting loss in revenues could force publishers to seek out cost-saving measures that hamper the user's experience, such as reduction in the quality of content, or to activate other revenue sources, e.g., via paywalls for their content. Given that policymakers also seek to nurture innovation and consumer wellbeing, these early insights suggest that it would be worthwhile for policymakers to evaluate whether the benefits of the GDPR are outweighed by its adverse effects on the industry. It is unclear to what extent regulators are taking this trade-off into account as they continue to expand privacy protections, by pushing transparency about targeted advertising (via the Digital Services Act), developing specific rules for electronic communication (via the ePrivacy Regulation) and limiting the power of large firms on the Internet, among them important publishers such as Google and Facebook (via the Digital Markets Act).

Our empirical study outlined that the online advertising industry is very complex. For example, on average, each publisher collaborates with 278 vendors. A justified question might be whether such a large number of collaborations is necessary. Yet, even cutting them down by 50% would leave each publisher with many vendors. As researchers in business and economics, we prefer efficient markets. Auctions, such as those used to sell online ads, represent a mechanism that is likely to make markets relatively efficient. Keeping those auctions certainly requires collaborating with a relatively large number of other firms.

As a result, we conclude that online advertising is and will remain a complex market. Accordingly, establishing a standardized set of procedures for GDPR compliance is likely to be in the interest of all market participants, including users. For example, standardized permissions for certain processing activities concerning personal data are likely to facilitate and improve users' decisions. The involvement of regulators in such standardization processes seems desirable. It would give users a strong voice and reduce firms' uncertainty concerning compliance with the GDPR and other legal requirements, such as the upcoming ePrivacy regulation.

Finding a good solution for privacy-preserving online advertising is a societal problem. If online advertising were to stop completely, the biggest losers would be publishers, not advertisers. Advertisers would suffer but spend their advertising budget elsewhere, e.g., on TV advertising. Publishers, however, would no longer be able to gain any income from selling online advertising slots. Consequently, publishers would either be forced to go out of business, reduce their content, or charge for content. Charging for content requires introducing paywalls, from which users with low income would likely suffer the most. As low income often correlates with lower education, these users might be lured by websites with low-quality content, in an extreme case, even fake news websites.

Though the scenario of a "slippery slope" from privacy protection to the failure of the digital publishing industry and the spread of fake news is admittedly somewhat extreme, it nevertheless serves to illustrate the key premise of this book: the idea that initiatives to protect user privacy should also consider other consequences, such as the economic and societal costs outlined above. We hope that our book enhances readers' understanding of the online advertising industry and the effects of privacy laws on this industry—and that, as a result, it contributes to a fruitful and open-minded discussion of how best to implement online consumer privacy.

11

References

Ada, Sila, Nadia Abou Nabout, and Elea McDonnell Feit (2022), "Context Information can Increase Revenue in Ad Auctions: Evidence from a Policy Change," *Journal of Marketing Research*, forthcoming.

Aguirre, E., D. Mahr, D. Grewal, K. D. Ruyter, and M. Wetzels (2015), "Unraveling the Personalization Paradox: The Effect of Information Collection and Trust-Building Strategies on Online Advertisement Effectiveness," *Journal of Retailing*, 91 (1), 34–59.

Athey, Susan, Christian Catalini, and Catherine Tucker (2017), "The Digital Privacy Paradox: Small Money, Small Costs, Small Talk." Working Paper.

Beke, Frank T., Felix Eggers, and Peter C. Verhoef (2018), "Consumer Informational Privacy: Current Knowledge and Research Directions," *Foundations and Trends in Marketing*, 11 (1), 1-71.

Bleier, Alexander and Maik Eisenbeiss (2015), "Personalized Online Advertising Effectiveness: The Interplay of What, When, and Where," *Marketing Science*, 34 (5), 669-88.

Bleier, Alexander, Avi Goldfarb, and Catherine. E. Tucker (2020), "Consumer Privacy and the Future of Data-Based Innovation and Marketing," *International Journal of Research in Marketing*, 37 (3), 466-80.

Board, Simon (2009), "Revealing Information in Auctions: the Allocation Effect," *Economic Theory*, 38 (1), 125-35.

Boerman, Sophie C., Sanne Kruikemeier, and Frederik J. Zuiderveen Borgesius (2017), "Online Behavioral Advertising: A Literature Review and Research Agenda," *Journal of Advertising*, 46 (3), 363-76.

Celis, L. Elisa, Sayash Kapoor, Farnood Salehi, and Nisheeth K. Vishnoi (2019), "Controlling Polarization in Personalization: An Algorithmic Framework," in FAT* '19: Proceedings of the Conference on Fairness, Accountability, and Transparency.

Chen, Jianqing and Jan Stallaert (2014), "An Economic Analysis of Online Advertising Using Behavioral Targeting," *MIS Quarterly*, 38 (2), 429-49.

Cristal, Gergory (2014), Ad Serving Technology. Understand the Marketing Revelation that Commercialized the Internet. Self-Publishing.

Datenschutzbehörde (2019), „Bescheid: Datenschutzbehörde entscheidet über die Datenschutzbeschwerde des Peter A*** (Beschwerdeführer) vom 04. Juni 2018 gegen die N*Mediengesellschaft m.b.H. (Beschwerdegegnerin) wegen Verletzung im Recht auf Geheimhaltung," in DSB-D122.974/0001-DSB/2019 vom 20.8.2019. https://www.ris.bka.gv.at/Dokumente/Dsk/DSBT_20190820_DSB_D122_974_0001_DSB_2019_00/DSBT_20190820_DSB_D122_974_0001_DSB_2019_00.html.

Degeling, M., C. Utz, C. Lentzsch, H. Hosseini, F. Schaub, and Holz; T. (2019), "We Value Your Privacy ... Now Take Some Cookies: Measuring the GDPR's Impact on Web Privacy," in 26th Annual Network and Distributed System Security Symposium, Internet Society.

Enge, Eric (2021), "Mobile vs. Desktop Usage in 2020," [available at https://www.perficient.com/insights/research-hub/mobile-vs-desktop-usage].

European Commission (2021), "Digital Markets Act: Ensuring Fair and Open Digital Markets," [available at https://ec.europa.eu/commission/presscorner/detail/en/QANDA_20_2349].

European Data Protection Board (2020), "Guidelines 05 / 2020 on Consent under Regulation 2016/679 (Version 1.1, Adopted on 4 May, 2020)." https://edpb.europa.eu/sites/default/files/files/file1/edpb_guidelines_202005_consent_en.pdf.

Gradow, Lisa and Ramona Greiner (2021), Quick Guide Consent-Management. Einwilligungen marketingoptimiert und DSGVO-konform einholen, verwalten und dokumentieren. Heidelberg: SpringerGabler.

Gross, Ralph and Alessandro Acquisti (2005), "Information Revelation and Privacy in Online Social Networks." WPES '05: Proceedings of the 2005 ACM Workshop on Privacy in the Electronic Society.

Ho, Shuk Ying and David Bodoff (2014), "The Effects of Web Personalization on User Attitude and Behavior," *MIS Quarterly*, 38 (2), 487-520.

Hsiao, Sissie (2020), "How our Display Buying Platforms Share Revenue with Publishers," in Blog Post on Google Ad Manager. https://blog.google/products/admanager/display-buying-share-revenue-publishers/.

IAB (2020), "AdEx Benchmark 2019." Report.

IAB (2021), "Internet Advertising Revenue Report. Full Year 2020 Results." Report.

IAB Europe (2021a), "ePrivacy Regulation: The Key Questions Answered," [available at https://datadrivenadvertising.eu/impact-of-eprivacy-regulation/].

IAB Europe (2021b), "IAB Europe, TCF and NOYB's War On Cookie Banners," [available at https://iabeurope.eu/blog/iab-europe-tcf-and-noybs-war-on-cookie-banners].

Information Commissioner's Office (2019), "Update Report into Adtech and Real Time Bidding."

Janssen, Rebecca, Reinhold Kesler, Michael Kummer, and Joel Waldfogel (2021), "GDPR and the Lost Generation of Innovative Apps," *Working Paper*.

Johnson, Garrett A., Scott Shriver, and Shaoyin Du (2020), "Consumer Privacy Choice in Online Advertising: Who Opts Out and at What Cost to Industry?," *Marketing Science*, 39 (1), 33-51.

Jürgensmeier, Lukas and Bernd Skiera (2022), "Measuring Fair Competition on Digital Platforms," *Working Paper, Goethe University Frankfurt*

Kosorin, Dominik (2016), Introduction to Programmatic Advertising. Self-Publishing.

Kraft, Lennart, Klaus M. Miller, and Bernd Skiera (2022), "Privacy and the Prevalence of Inconsistencies in Third-Party Consumer Profiling on the Internet," *Working Paper, Goethe University Frankfurt*.

Kulyk, Oksana, Nina Gerber, Annika Hilt, and Melanie Volkamer (2020), "Has the GDPR Hype Affected Users' Reaction to Cookie Disclaimers? ," *Journal of Cyber Security*, 6 (1), 1-14.

Lambrecht, Anja and Catherine Tucker (2013), "When Does Retargeting Work? Timing Information Specificity," *Journal of Marketing Research*, 50 (5), 561-76.

Laub, René, Klaus M. Miller, and Bernd Skiera (2022), "The Economic Value of User Tracking and Behavioral Targeting for Publishers," *Working Paper, Goethe University Frankfurt*.

Lee, Kuang-Chih, Ali Jalali, and Ali Dasdan (2013), "Real Time Bid Optimization with Smooth Budget Delivery in Online Advertising." Proceedings of the 19th ACM Conference on Knowledge Discovery and Data Mining (KDD'13).

Levin, Jonathan and Paul Milgrom (2010), "Online Advertising: Heterogeneity and Conflation in Market Design," *American Economic Review: Papers & Proceedings*, 100 (May), 603-07.

Lischka, Helena Maria and Peter Kenning (2020), Need for Digital Privacy – Ansatzpunkt der marktorientierten Unternehmensführung für Innovationen in der digitalen

Wirtschaft!?,' in Handbuch Digitale Wirtschaft, edited by T. Kollmann: Springer, 2020: 1209-1229.

Lukic, Karlo, Klaus M. Miller, and Bernd Skiera (2022), "The Impact of the General Data Protection Regulation (GDPR) on Online Tracking," *Working Paper, Goethe University Frankfurt*.

Luma Partners (2021), "Display Lumascape." https://lumapartners.com/content/lumascapes/display-ad-tech-lumascape/.

Martin, Kelly D. and Patrick E. Murphy (2017), "The Role of Data Privacy in Marketing," *Journal of the Academy of Marketing Science*, 45 (2), 135–55.

Miller, Klaus M. and Bernd Skiera (2022), "Economic Consequences of Online Tracking Restrictions," *Working Paper, Goethe University Frankfurt*.

Müller-Tribbensee, Timo, Klaus Miller, and Bernd Skiera (2022), "Consent-or-Pay Walls," *Working Paper, Goethe University Frankfurt*.

Neumann, Nico, Catherine. E. Tucker, and Timothy Whitfield (2019), "Frontiers: How Effective is Third-Party Consumer Profiling? Evidence from Field Studies," *Marketing Science*, 38 (6), 918-26.

Norberg, Patricia A., Daniel R. Horne, and David A. Horne (2007), "The Privacy Paradox: Personal Information Disclosure Intentions versus Behaviors," *Journal of Consumer Affairs*, 41 (1), 100-26.

O'Neil, Cathy (2016), Weapons of Math Destruction: How Big Data Increases Inequality and Threatens Democracy: Crown.

Owen, Malcolm (2021), "Ireland Fails in Tackling Big Tech Privacy Complaints," *Apple Insiders, https://appleinsider.com/articles/21/09/13/ireland-fails-in-tackling-big-tech-privacy-complaints, Sep 13, 2021*.

Peukert, Christian, Stefan Bechtold, Michail Batikas, and Tobias Kretschmer (2022), "Regulatory Spillovers and Data Governance: Evidence from the GDPR," *Marketing Science*, forthcoming.

Pew Research Center (2019), "Americans and Privacy: Concerned, Confused and Feeling Lack of Control Over Their Personal Information," (accessed 20.01.2021, [available at https://www.pewresearch.org/internet/2019/11/15/americans-and-privacy-concerned-confused-and-feeling-lack-of-control-over-their-personal-information/].

Pidgeon, David (2016), "Where did the Money Go? Guardian Buys its Own Ad Inventory," in Mediatel News. https://mediatel.co.uk/news/2016/10/04/where-did-the-money-go-guardian-buys-its-own-ad-inventory/.

Presthus, W. and H. Sørum (2018), "Are Consumers Concerned About Privacy? An Online Survey Emphasizing the General Data Protection Regulation," *Procedia Computer Science*, 138, 603–11.

Roth, Yannig (2020), "Google Joining TCF v2… Here's What it Means for Publishers," [available at https://blog.didomi.io/en/google-joining-tcf-v2-what-it-means-for-publishers].

Ryan, Johnny (2018), "Report from Dr. Johnny Ryan – Behavioural Advertising and Personal Data." https://brave.com/wp-content/uploads/2018/09/Behavioural-advertising-and-personal-data.pdf.

Ryan, Johnny (2020), "Response to Consultation regarding 'Online Platforms and Digital Advertising'." https://brave.com/competition-internal-external/.

Sahni, Navdeep S., Sridhar Narayanan, and Kirthi Kalyanam (2019), "An Experimental Investigation of the Effects of Retargeted Advertising: The Role of Frequency and Timing," *Journal of Marketing Research*, 56 (3), 401-18.

Sanchez-Rola, I., M. Dell'Amico, P. Kotzias, D. Balzarotti, L. Bilge, P.-A. Vervier, and I. Santos (2019), "Can I Opt Out Yet? GDPR and the Global Illusion of Cookie Control," in ACM ASIA Conference on Computer and Communications Security. New York, USA.

Schmitt, Julia (2021), "The Illusion of Control: Control and Convenience on Consent Banners," *Working Paper, Goethe University Frankfurt*.

Schmitt, Julia, Klaus M. Miller, and Bernd Skiera (2022), "The Impact of Privacy Laws on Online User Behavior," *Working Paper, Goethe University Frankfurt*.

Shiller, Benjamin, Joel Waldfogel, and Johnny Ryan (2018), "The Effect of Ad Blocking on Website Traffic and Quality," *Journal of Economics*, 49 (1), 43-64.

Trusov, Michael, Liye Ma, and Zainab Jamal (2016), "Crumbs of the Cookie: User Profiling in Customer-Base Analysis and Behavioral Targeting," *Marketing Science*, 35 (3), 405-26.

Voisin, Gabriel, Ruth Boardman, Simon Assion, Clara Clark Nevola, Lupe Sampedro, and Ester Vidal (2019), "ICO, CNIL, German and Spanish DPA revised Cookies Guidelines: Convergence and Divergence," *Report, https://iapp.org/resources/article/ico-and-cnil-revised-cookie-guidelines-convergence-and-divergence/*.

Wang, Jun, Weinan Zhang, and Shuai Yuan (2017), "Display Advertising with Real-Time Bidding (RTB) and Behavioural Targeting." arXiv:1610.03013v2 [cs.GT] on July 15, 2017.

Westin, A. F. (1967), Privacy and Freedom. New York: Athenaeum.

Wieringa, Jaap, K.P. Kannan, Xiao Ma, Thomas Reutterer, Hans Risseladaa, and Bernd Skiera (2021), "Data Analytics in a Privacy-Concerned World," *Journal of Business Research*, 122, 915-25.

Wurmser, Yoram (2021), "The Majority of Americans' Mobile Time Spent Takes Place in Apps," [available at https://www.emarketer.com/content/the-majority-of-americans-mobile-time-spent-takes-place-in-apps].

Yan, Shunyao, Klaus M. Miller, and Bernd Skiera (2022), "How Does the Adoption of Ad Blockers Affect News Consumption?," *Journal of Marketing Research*, forthcoming.

Yuan, Shuai, Jun Wang, and Xiaoxue Zhao (2013), "Real-time Bidding for Online Advertising: Measurement and Analysis," in Proceedings of the Seventh International Workshop on Data Mining for Online Advertising. Chicago, Illinois: ACM.

12

Glossary

A/B Testing: An experiment to assess the impact of two (or even more) different versions of a system, such as a website or an app.

Adblocker: Refers to software programs, often browser extensions, that users can use to block ads.

Ad Impression: Displaying an online ad once on a publisher's property, such as a website or an app. The number of ad impressions refers to how often an online ad was shown.

Ad Exchange: A marketplace where advertisers or demand-side platforms purchase the opportunity to show ad impressions to users from publishers or supply-side platforms.

Ad Inventory: The collection of ad slots of a publisher at a specific point in time.

Ad Server: Web server (i.e., a computer) that stores advertising content (e.g., banner ads) and sends the specific ad for display to the publisher's property.

Ad Slot: A specific space on a publisher's property, such as a website or an app, where an ad appears. The ad slot has characteristics, such as the size of the ad or the location on the publisher's property.

Advanced Data Protection Control (ADPC): A tool initiated by NOYB that considers user privacy preferences and reduces the annoyance of repetitive cookie banners.

Advertiser: A firm that advertises an offering.

Ad Wastage: Ads shown to consumers who are not interested in the offer to which the ad refers.

Anonymous Data: Any data that neither directly nor indirectly identify natural persons.

Application Programming Interface (API): A connection that enables computer programs to exchange information.

Audience: A collection of consumers that share a particular characteristic such as a demographic, interest, or purchase intention.

Attribution Modeling: The process of assessing which ads (or marketing actions) contributed how much toward a specific goal (e.g., purchasing an offering).

Behavioral targeting: Using information about the users' behavior (e.g., their previous browsing behavior) to show specific ads. In an extreme setting, each user would see a different ad.

Bid Request: The call of the seller in an auction to potential buyers to place a bid. The ad exchange usually asks advertisers to place a bid for purchasing one ad impression in online advertising.

Browser Extension: A software extension for a browser providing additional functionalities to the user, such as "Ghostery," which represents an adblocker.

California Consumer Privacy Act (CCPA): The privacy law applicable to California became effective on January 1st, 2020.

Click-Through Rate: The number of times users click on an ad divided by the number of ad impressions, i.e., the number of times the advertiser showed the ad. The click-through rate describes the share of users who clicked on an ad.

Consent: Under the GDPR, it is one of the two most common legal bases for personal data processing for online advertising. It describes the active permission of a user that the firm can process personal data. Loosely speaking, it represents a user's opt-in for personal data processing.

Consent Log: A list of all decisions of user permission decisions regarding the processing of personal data.

Consent Management Platform (CMP): An actor of the online advertising market that helps publishers to collect users' permission for personal data processing activities.

Consent Rate: The number of times users consented to personal data processing divided by the number of times users consent to or deny personal data processing. So, it is the share of users providing consent. The consent rate can differ across platforms, websites, and apps.

Consumer Privacy: The degree of users' control over their data and personal data processing.

Contextual Targeting: The approach to show consumers ads based upon the context of the publisher's property they currently visit.

Cookies: A small piece of data sent from a server to a browser and stored in the browser on the user's device.

Cookie Banner: A pop-up display on a publisher's property that informs the users about personal data processing activities and asks for permission for personal data processing.

Cookie Banner Layer: A cookie banner might consist of one or more layers. The user sees the first layer immediately but must make one or more clicks to see the second or other layers. Usually, the first layer provides fewer details than the other layers.

Cookie Paywalls: A publisher forcing a user to choose between (i) providing permission for personal data processing or (ii) paying for not providing permission for personal data processing.

Data Breach: A situation where non-authorized entities have access to (personal) data.

Data Controller: A term under the GDPR that describes a firm that decides why and how to process personal data.

Data Processor: A term under the GDPR that describes a firm that processes personal data on behalf of the data controller.

Data Protection Authority (DPA): Independent public authorities supervising the application of the data protection law through investigative and corrective powers.

Data Management Platform (DMP): An actor of the online advertising market that supports the collection, storage, and usage of data.

Demand-side Platform (DSP): An actor of the online advertising market that helps advertisers to purchase ad impressions on ad exchanges.

Digital Fingerprinting: The process of identifying a user based on the specific configuration of the user's device.

Digital Markets Act (DMA): A proposal of the European Union aiming to ensure competition in European digital markets.

Digital Services Act (DSA): A proposal of the European Union aiming to enhance, among others, the transparency of online advertising and to avoid illegal consent and disinformation.

Display Advertising: A graphical ad on a publisher's property, such as a website or an app.

Feature: A term under the Transparency and Consent Framework (TCF) that refers to the means (e.g., "Link different devices" to determine that two or more devices belong to the same user) to reach a specific goal.

First-party Data: The kind of data a firm collects on its property, such as a website or an app.

Frequency Capping: An approach to limit the number of times a specific user sees the same ad.

General Data Protection Regulation (GDPR): A privacy law of the European Union applicable to all European firms and all firms processing personal data of European citizens adopted on May 25, 2016, and enacted on May 25, 2018.

Global Vendor List (GVL): A term under the Transparency and Consent Framework (TCF) that describes the list of vendors participating in the Transparency and Consent Framework (TCF).

Interactive Advertising Bureau (IAB): An association of digital marketing and advertising firms. Interactive Advertising Bureau Europe refers to the European part of the association.

ID: A unique combination of letters or numbers that identify an entity such as a user or a cookie.

Legal Basis: Under the GDPR, it describes the legal argument for an activity processing personal data.

Legitimate Interest: Under the GDPR, it is one of the two most common legal bases for personal data processing for online advertising. It weighs the firm's interest in personal data processing against the user's interest in not processing it. Loosely speaking, it represents the user's opt-out approach for personal data processing.

Legitimate Interest Assessment (LIA): The assessment between a firm's interest in personal data processing and a user's interest in not processing it.

Local Storage: Storage in the user's browser.

None Of Your Business (NOYB): A non-profit organization aiming to enforce user rights on the internet.

Opt-in: Refers to a proactive decision of the user to provide consent for personal data processing.

Opt-out: Refers to a proactive decision of the user to not provide consent for personal data processing.

Personal Data: Refers to any information relating to an identified or identifiable natural person ('data subject'); an identifiable natural person can be identified, directly or indirectly, in particular by reference to an identifier such as a name, an identification number, location data, an online identifier or to one or more factors specific to the physical, physiological, genetic, mental, economic, cultural or social identity of that natural person.

Piggyback Tracker: A tracker that hides within another tracker, aiming to track consumers across the internet.

Premium Publisher: A publisher with a property, such as a website or an app, that has a good brand reputation, thus offering an attractive space to show ads.

Personal Data Processing: Refers to any operation or set of operations which is performed on personal data or sets of personal data, whether or not by automated means, such as collection, recording, organization, structuring, storage, adaptation or alteration, retrieval, consultation, use, disclosure by transmission, dissemination or otherwise making available, alignment or combination, restriction, erasure or destruction.

Personal Information Management Services (PIMS): A software automatically detecting and responding to data requests, such as consent requests. In such a case, the user of the software only needs to provide the user's privacy preferences once in the PIMS and update it if the privacy preferences of the user change. Such an update then automatically notifies and updates all other actors that process the user's data.

Profiling: Often, actors of the online advertising industry use the data collected about a user (e.g., the browsing behavior) to derive insights into the user's demographics, interests, and purchase intentions. This process is called profiling.

Programmatic Advertising: The automatic selling of an ad impression. It often refers to the publisher selling one ad impression in real-time in an auction to an advertiser. It is also referred to as real-time bidding (RTB), real-time advertising (RTA), or programmatic buying.

Pseudonymous Data: Data that does not directly but indirectly identify natural persons.

Publisher: The owner of the property on the internet, which users visit. In the advertising context, the publisher represents the seller of the space where users see ads.

Publisher Restriction: A term under the Transparency and Consent Framework (TCF) that describes the publisher's decision upon the purpose and the legal basis for processing personal data. It restricts the vendor's choice of a purpose or a legal basis.

PUR Model: Another label for "Cookie Paywalls," see Cookie Paywalls

Purpose of Personal Data Processing: The goal of personal data processing (e.g., "Create a personalized ads profile" to profile users) that the data controller aims to achieve via a specific feature or means.

Purpose Specification: Refers to the process of identifying legitimate purposes for personal data processing and specifying these purposes in a clear (explicit) manner.

Real-time Bidding: Another label for "Programmatic Advertising." See Programmatic Advertising.

Recency Capping: An approach to only show a user the same ad again if a minimum amount of time has passed.

Retargeting: Also referred to as remarketing or behavioral retargeting. It uses information about the previous behavior of the user to target the user with an ad that is specific to the previous behavior. For example, retargeting reminds a user of a product that the user put into the shopping basket but did not purchase.

Search Engine Ads: Ads that occur on search engines such as Google or Bing.

Second-party Data: The kind of data a firm receives from another firm that belongs to the same owner.

Special Feature: A term under the Transparency and Consent Framework (TCF) that describes a more privacy intrusive feature that a firm can only use if the user provides consent.

Special Purpose: A term under the Transparency and Consent Framework (TCF) that describes a technically necessary purpose so that a firm can serve ads.

Stack: A term under the Transparency and Consent Framework (TCF) that describes the grouping of (Special) Purposes and (Special) Features to decrease the number of user decisions for personal data processing.

Supervising Authority: An authority that oversees the compliance of firms with privacy laws such as the GDPR.

Supply-side Platform (SSP): An actor of the online advertising market that publishers use to sell the opportunity to show ad impressions via ad exchanges.

Targeting: The process of showing ads to a group of users that fulfill specific criteria.

Third-party Data: The kind of data a firm receives from another firm that does not belong to the same owner.

Tracking: The process of collecting data about users.

Tracking-Free Ads Coalition: An association of European politicians, citizens, and firms aiming to end tracking on the internet.

Transparency and Consent Framework (TCF): An industry initiative developed by IAB Europe assisting firms in addressing the challenges of getting and managing user permission for personal data processing.

TCF Purpose: A term under the Transparency and Consent Framework (TCF) that describes the pre-defined goals of personal data processing.

TC String: A term under the Transparency and Consent Framework (TCF) that describes how to store the user's consent decision.

Verification Provider: An actor of the online advertising industry that verifies that an ad appears on the correct publisher's property, such as a particular website or app.

Vendor: A term under the Transparency and Consent Framework (TCF) that describes an actor of the online advertising industry. Usually, these actors provide technologies to either advertisers or publishers.

13

Information about the Authors

13.1 Bernd Skiera

Bernd Skiera (skiera@wiwi.uni-frankfurt.de) is a chaired professor of electronic commerce at Goethe University Frankfurt (Germany), a Professorial Fellow at Deakin University (Australia) and a member of the board of the EFL-Data Science Institute and the Schmalenbach-Gesellschaft. His research interests are consumer privacy, marketing analytics, data-driven marketing, electronic commerce, online advertising, SalesTech, MarTech and marketing automation. He received an ERC Advanced Grant to conduct research on consumer privacy on the Internet.

13.2 Klaus Miller

Klaus Miller (millerk@hec.fr) is an assistant professor of quantitative marketing and Hi! Paris chairholder for the study of data science and artificial intelligence in business and society at HEC Paris (France). During his Ph.D. and as a Post-Doctoral Scholar he has been visiting the Wharton School at the University of Pennsylvania and the Graduate School of Business at Stanford University. His research interests meet at the interface of empirical quantitative marketing, management economics, and information systems. Specifically, his research concerns pricing, advertising, and customer management topics in the digital economy. Recently, Klaus has developed an research interest in online consumer privacy.

13.3 Yuxi Jin

Yuxi Jin (y.jin@wiwi.uni-frankfurt.de) is a doctoral student at Goethe University Frankfurt (Germany). Her research interests are consumer privacy and regulation, online advertising, and data analytics.

13.4 Lennart Kraft

Lennart Kraft (lennart.kraft@wiwi.uni-frankfurt.de) is a doctoral student in Quantitative Economics at Goethe University Frankfurt (Germany) and senior data manager at Financial Research Data Infrastructure of Leibniz Institute for Financial Research SAFE. His research interests comprise quantitative economics, online marketing, and consumer privacy, focusing on the interplay of privacy and profits in online advertising markets.

13.5 René Laub

René Laub (rlaub@wiwi.uni-frankfurt.de) is a doctoral student at Goethe University Frankfurt (Germany). His research interests are at the interface of marketing and information systems research, focusing on consumer privacy, digital marketing, and MarTech.

13.6 Julia Schmitt

Julia Schmitt (schmitt@wiwi.uni-frankfurt.de) was a doctoral student at Goethe University Frankfurt (Germany). Her research interests are consumer privacy, privacy regulations, consent management and data analytics.

CPSIA information can be obtained
at www.ICGtesting.com
Printed in the USA
BVHW021540250422
635266BV00002B/11